Classic Civil Aircraft:2

BOEING 707

Classic Civil Aircraft: 2

BOEING 707

ALAN J. WRIGHT

LIBYAN ARAB AIRLINES

LONDON

IAN ALLAN LTD

Contents

First published 1990

ISBN 0 7110 1910 X

© Ian Allan Ltd 1990

Published by Ian Allan Ltd, Shepperton, Surrey; and printed by Ian Allan Printing Ltd at their works at Coombelands in Runnymede, England

Front cover:
A Boeing 707-331C is seen here in the livery of TWA. *Boeing*

Rear cover:
Boeing plant view of 707s on the flight test line undergoing servicing checks: from front to rear the aircraft are N762PA, N747TW, N746TW, N7226U, N720V (Pacific Northern) and an unidentified aircraft for El Al. *Boeing*

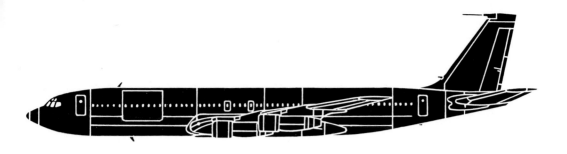

Preface

When the Dash Eighty was rolled out in May 1954 few people could have foreseen the effect that it was to have on the development of air transport. Its 707 offspring has undoubtedly become a classic aircraft, not only because of its own outstanding career, but because of the subsequent designs that owe so much to this pioneer of the 1950s. Decades later the four-engined jet is still in regular service in many parts of the world and is likely to continue for many more years.

Boeing had not been in any hurry to enter the commercial market with a jet-powered airliner, partly because there was a certain amount of resistance to the idea from the travelling public, but also because of its continuing association with bombers. Airlines themselves were still happy with the piston-engined types of the day and in any case were expecting the next generation to be powered by turboprops despite the success of the early Comets. While there was still the disadvantage of propellers, most of the benefits of turbojets were present including the attraction of much improved economics. In the event progress quickly bypassed this phase as the Boeing and Douglas products took command of the long-haul work.

As with many of its generation, the 707 always tested the full-scale deflection facility of decibel-meters with enthusiasm until the advent of noise restrictions. These could have ended the type's usefulness, but hush-kitting proved successful and so the surviving 707s received a new lease of life. Smoke trailing behind the aircraft was also a familiar feature, the quantity seemingly varying with individual carriers. Since the type's introduction coincided with the demise of steam in the UK, it was

almost as if some of the redundant firemen had remustered as flight engineers.

With the arrival of the wide-bodies in the early 1970s, so the 707s slowly moved off the trunk routes. Many were configured with high-density seating and used on inclusive tour flights thereby playing a large part in the introduction of the masses to modern air transport. As the years progressed, not only did operators from the Third World find it a practical proposition to employ single 707s on freight work, but the example was followed by carriers from emerging countries even further down the league table of nations. Some gave the impression that the aircraft had in fact directly replaced the mule or camel and that the handling characteristics were similar.

In addition to its valuable contribution to the commercial scene, the 707 airframe has proved an extremely versatile platform for military use. Some of the modifications necessary to install electronic equipment have produced swollen noses or other painful-looking protuberances elsewhere. Probably the most startling addition to the structure was the circular piece of hardware planted on the rear fuselage. It seems highly likely that the combination of this expensive gadget and the 707 will be flying for many years on its peace-keeping missions. After all, if an early-warning device cannot survive there is little chance for the rest!

Grateful thanks are extended to Boeing's Public Relations Division and its UK representative, Dick Kenny, for help given during the preparation of this book.

Alan J. Wright

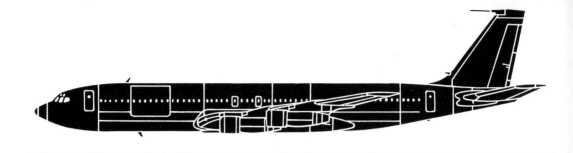

Origins

A chance trip aloft on Independence Day, 1914, was responsible for the creation of a company destined to play a large part in both civil and military aviation history. It was at Seattle that the 32-year-old William Boeing took to the air on board the joy-riding Curtiss seaplane, an experience which convinced him that he had to continue this association with flying.

Hitherto wood had played a large part in his life, because not only did he own a timber company but also a furniture factory and boat yard, all of which were very successful in their own right. It was therefore not entirely surprising that with his flair and enterprise, his involvement in this new activity was enthusiastic. At that time of course, flying did not feature very highly in the public's scale of priorities, most people preferring to leave this unnatural impersonation of birds to those with no burning ambition for longevity. While Boeing was a far-sighted optimist, it is unlikely that even in his wildest dreams did he foresee what an impact his future company would have on world events.

After his brief excursion aloft the next step was obvious to the excited aeronaut — he would build his own machine. Boeing already shared a mutual interest in aviation with a US Navy officer acquaintance named Conrad Westervelt, so the latter was persuaded to design an aircraft as a joint venture. He had no knowledge of the art, but by sheer determination the handicap was overcome to produce the B&W Model 1, the name derived from the initials of the two partners. Construction of the machine was split between two separate locations, with most of the manpower originating from the furniture factory.

By June 1916 the first machine had been completed and awaited its inaugural sortie. In those days this constituted an adventure because there

Above:
Although William Boeing was responsible for his company's early development, his resignation ended active participation as early as 1934. However during World War 2 he acted as an advisor and later was present at Renton for the roll-out of the Dash Eighty in May 1954, two years or so before his death in September 1956. *Boeing Archives*

were no facilities for thoroughly proving the airframe's design prior to flight. At least the team had wide experience with boat hulls, so there seemed every chance that the two-seat seaplane would at least float. This indeed proved to be the case and as a bonus, with Boeing himself at the

controls, it also flew. Remarkably there were very few modifications required, so it was not long before the machine was offered to the US Navy in the hope of securing an order. Despite favourable comments, the military rejected the B&W 1 but at least it had provided Boeing with practical experience and certainly the setback did not deter him from continuing his work.

To coincide with these events, the business became known as Pacific Aero Products, but after only a few months with this title it was changed once again to become The Boeing Airplane Company. This became possible because during this period the original partnership was reduced by half when Westervelt's military employers decided that it was not unreasonable to expect him to concentrate on their needs in the future. Accordingly he was posted to the east coast of America in readiness for action should the country enter the European war. Boeing therefore found himself in need of a new designer, a profession still with few active members. Nevertheless he managed to secure the services of T. Wong, a Chinese gentleman with an impressive reputation.

From his drawing board came the Model C in 1917, basically another float plane but one which could be adapted for land operations without any undue difficulty. After a hazardous first flight several major changes were made to the design before it was declared good enough to market. Once again the Navy was invited to evaluate the machine and this time Boeing's salesmen pilots impressed the customer so effectively that an order for 50 aircraft was received. Success indeed, but somewhat marred by the resignation of the Oriental designer despite having proved that one Wong could make a right even if the proverb claimed it to be beyond the scope of two!

It was not the best of moments to lose such an important member of the company. To avoid such an inconvenient occurrence in the future a search began for two senior staff members who would be prepared to remain loyal to Boeing but at the same time be top of their class. By bringing stability to the upper management, those recruited during the drive thereafter played a major part in the successful growth of the manufacturer through the years.

In addition to producing its own Model C, Boeing was also entrusted with the building of other types as a sub-contractor during the latter stages of World War 1. Although the work ensured a steady income, for some members of the staff commercial aviation was seen to be the key to the future. Such thoughts had to be abandoned following the Armistice in November 1918 when the expected military cutbacks provided the civil market with an abundance of surplus aircraft. Naturally contracts were also cancelled, a fact which had a serious effect on Boeing's financial status.

Fortunately the company still had its furniture production so this source of income was used to support the much-reduced but still active aircraft division through the lean times. Several new designs were produced but none attracted any interest from the military, until in the early 1920s Boeing received a valuable contract to modernise some de Havilland DH4s. Not only did it provide

employment for the dwindling staff but it also presented the opportunity for some original work on new aircraft for the Army Air Corps. Throughout the decade a series of biplane fighters, bombers and trainers were designed and built with varied success, while the company's association with water continued with the appearance of several flying boats, none of which were developed to any great extent. More significant was the completion of Boeing's first commercial machine, designated the Model 40.

Conceived to meet a Post Office contract for the Chicago-San Francisco sector, the single-engined biplane was able to accommodate two passengers in addition to the required 1,000lb of mail. It was this capability for carrying fare-paying human cargo that enabled Boeing to undercut the competition by submitting a bid that even the Post Office thought too low. Nevertheless, the operation was launched and was eventually able to report that 1,863 travellers had used the service during the first year. With the fare for the journey set at $400, it

Above:
Essentially a mailplane, the Model 40 could also carry two passengers in the forward cabin. *Boeing*

Above right:
Several versions of the Model 40 were produced, the 40B having a cabin capable of accommodating four passengers. The final 20 machines built also featured a cowl for the Pratt & Whitney Hornet. *Boeing*

Right:
Even in 1927 the Boeing plant had established a production line upon which both PW-9 fighters and the civilian Model 40 were built. *Boeing*

produced some very welcome income for the expanding company.

Encouraged by this achievement, steps were almost immediately taken to develop something more ambitious, particularly since several large transports already existed both in the US and Europe. In those days the time from drawing board to completion was often very speedy as was the

Above:
One of the Model 80As operated by Boeing Air Transport, NC226M was finished in grey with green and orange trim on both fuselage and fin.
Boeing Archives

case with the Model 80 which appeared barely a year after work began. It was an advanced three-engined machine with many original features included in its substantial frame. A heated cabin could contain 14 passengers while the crew of two were isolated in their own position high in the nose behind the centre power unit. Such previously unheard of items such as reading lamps, leather upholstery, hot and cold running water and air ventilation were thoughtfully provided. Previously the two latter facilities were only available while

Below:
Originally built as a Model 200, NC725W was converted into a Model 221A to make its first flight on 6 May 1930. *Boeing Archives*

flying in a standard open cockpit in rain. Such was progress. Strangely enough pilots were not impressed by an enclosed compartment since they preferred an unobscured view from their lofty perch.

Although popular, sales of the Model 80 were disappointing and would have been insufficient to keep the fast expanding company in business without an alternative source of revenue which was, as always, the government. It continued to prove a valuable customer with both Army and Navy air arms regularly placing orders for Boeing's new offerings, although all continued the biplane theme.

Towards the end of the 1920s a start was made on a revolutionary concept, an all-metal monoplane. First flown on 22 May 1930, the Model 200 Monomail possessed a low wing and retractable undercarriage while the single radial engine had been given a cowling intended to reduce drag as much as possible. Primarily it was intended as a fast mail carrier, but Boeing also included a cabin in the forward fuselage of a modified version (Model 221)

which was capable of accommodating up to eight passengers. Traditionally the pilot remained in the open air to the rear of the wing from which point vision was unobstructed. Ironically its advanced design was largely responsible for its failure to sell. In order to make full use of its capabilities a propeller with variable pitch was needed, but such a device still had to be developed.

Much had been learned with the 200; expertise which was expanded into a twin-engined bomber for the USAAC. Once again the outcome proved to be outstanding, its advanced technological features being vastly superior to those of the elderly types currently in service. Boeing was undoubtedly disappointed when it failed to win an order for its latest creation, especially since the Model 246 was officially designated B-9 for the duration of a lengthy period of evaluation. Probably the innovations incorporated were moving ahead too fast for the traditionalists, but the effort had not been wasted because later military designs of considerable importance benefited from this early research.

At the dawn of the 1930s there were already signs that there was an urgent need for rapid coast-to-coast transportation across the US. Even the fastest trains took three days for the journey so it was not a trip undertaken lightly. Towards the end of the 1920s a few airlines began a series of services using a mix of air and rail transport in an attempt to improve the situation. At least the method enabled the overall elapsed time to be reduced to 48hr. This interim solution ended in October 1930 when Transcontinental & Western Airlines (TWA) began through air services using the venerable Ford Tri-Motor, a thoroughly reliable machine but one which lacked many of the modern refinements.

In parallel with B-9 development work, Boeing had also been planning a new contender for the commercial market. It was a very advanced project, incorporating all the streamlining and anti-drag devices that were technically possible at the time. Other innovations included de-icing on both wing and tail surfaces plus an elevator and aileron trim-tab system. Identified as the Model 247, the twin-engined monoplane's cabin could accommodate 10 passengers in armchair seats set at a very comfortable 40in pitch. At the rear there was a toilet provided, while the presence of a galley complete with stewardess meant that there was the added bonus of refreshments during the journey.

It also marked the end of the open air life for the pilots because a modern style flight deck was provided in the nose. Until now there had been little regard to the effect of noise on the ears of the intrepid travellers. Apart from dispensing lumps of cotton wool or other suitably pliable material, operators could do little to alleviate the suffering. With the coming of the 247 this was not so. While still by no means reminiscent of a public library's reading room, nevertheless a serious attempt had at last been made to install some sound-proofing in the interior.

Hopes ran high at Seattle when United Air Lines ordered 60 aircraft even when it was still at the mock-up stage. It augured well for the type's prospects. First flown on 8 February 1933, a trouble-free test programme enabled the first example to enter service with United on 30 March. Amazingly by the end of June the airline had no fewer than 30 on strength and had already taken the record for the coast-to-coast schedule with a time of 19¾hr. In the face of this competition TWA had managed to trim its time for the same journey to 26¾hr, a reduction achieved by over-flying Kansas City en route. While this was a creditable performance by the Tri-Motors, it could only be a temporary expedient until more efficient equipment was available.

With Boeing's production committed to the large initial order, there was little chance of securing early delivery of the 247, so TWA looked for an alternative. It managed to interest Douglas in building a rival airliner, design of which started in earnest in September 1932. Not only did the new DC series include the same advanced features as the Boeing machine, but unlike the 247 it had the advantage of a 12-seat cabin unobstructed by the wing spar. Douglas had evolved a multi-cellular wing which could be integrated into the fuselage structure without intruding into the passenger area. When introduced to scheduled services in May 1934 the newcomer immediately began to collect an impressive array of records — mostly at the expense of the 247. United countered this challenge by updating its fleet with new interior decor, while Boeing for its part greatly improved its product's performance by fitting variable pitch propellers developed by Hamilton Standard, an associate company. This device had first been fitted to the aircraft entered in the 1934 England-Australia air race, but although it increased the cruising speed by 7mph the 247D was placed third — just behind the DC-2. Despite determined efforts to interest the airlines, few orders were forthcoming which meant that production ended after 75 had been built.

For almost two years the 247 had reigned supreme in the US and had played a large part in the development of modern air services. Unfortunately for the Boeing machine its wing spar discouraged any increase in capacity whereas Douglas and TWA modified the DC-2 to accommodate 14 passengers while the DC-3 could carry 21 in its extended cabin. Orders for the latter were received from far and wide while United valiantly battled on with its improved 247s. Finally even this faithful supporter of the type had to admit defeat by ordering a number of DC-3s for its high-intensity Los Angeles-San Francisco route.

Once again Boeing faced financial problems. Much had depended upon the success of the 247 but with no more sales the future looked rather bleak. The threat of unemployment loomed for many of the employees, but loyally they suggested staggering their hours so that the remaining work was equally shared. A reprieve was obtained with the award of a contract to design and build a new long range bomber for the Army Air Corps. Known as the XB-15, it became the largest aircraft to have been built in the US at the time of its first flight in October 1937. Only the prototype was produced but after evaluation by the military it went on to give valuable service, not as a bomber, but as a troop and cargo carrier throughout World War 2.

Even while the XB-15 was being conceived Boeing was also involved in tendering for a bomber capable of defending itself against aerial attacks. Known as the Model 299, and despite a fatal crash when under evaluation, the company was awarded a contract to produce a small batch of aircraft now identified as the B-17. It was quite a gamble because, as a private venture, funding had to come from the manufacturer's already depleted coffers. While the aircraft met the specification, experience proved it to be unsatisfactory when first used operationally. Learning from the lesson, Boeing introduced many changes until the final variants were far removed from the original design. Thousands of the 'Flying Fortress' saw service with the US forces and, together with the Liberator, played a major role in the day raids on Europe.

Meanwhile the expertise gained during the development of the B-15 was used to fulfil Boeing's ambition to remain in the commercial market. A Pan American requirement for a long range, large capacity flying boat interested the manufacturer sufficiently for it to submit proposals to the airline for such a machine. With the design accepted, a contract was received for six machines plus an option on a similar number. Delivery of the first half dozen Model 314s took place between January and June 1939 for service entry on the airline's Pacific and Atlantic routes.

There was a vast amount of room within the hull for cabins, lounges, dressing rooms and other luxury accommodation. It was an era when flying boats were considered the best solution for long distance travel especially since so much of the time was spent over water. For these flights only 34 passengers were carried but on short range sorties the total rose to 74 with a crew of 10. Undoubtedly it was a most agreeable method of transport but still beyond the reach of the vast majority. Although the war curtailed the type's operational life, the 314s were used throughout to good effect in all parts of the world. Sadly this valuable contribution did not bring continued support when hostilities had ended because by then landplanes were firmly in favour, which meant that by 1951 all survivors had been scrapped.

When the Model 247 was beaten by the Douglas DC series, in many respects it was probably beneficial to Boeing in the long term. Instead of a prolonged production run absorbing all

Some of the 10 Stratoliners built were purchased by the French carrier, Airnautic, after World War 2, one such specimen being F-BELY seen during a visit to Gatwick in September 1963. *G. W. Pennick*

the resources, the company was able to devote its full attention to research. High altitude flight was one aspect which attracted the manufacturer and although the B-17 was designed for just such a purpose, the crew relied upon oxygen. This was clearly not a suitable arrangement for passenger-carrying aircraft, yet the advantages of flying over the more turbulent lower level conditions were obvious. There was also the safety factor to consider because no longer would airliners have to thread their way through mountain ranges, but instead could fly over the top.

The answer was a pressurised cabin, a device in fact first flown by Lockheed in its 1937 vintage XC-37. Boeing was also proceeding along similar lines, but on a much larger scale. An airliner version of the B-17 was planned, but while using the same wings, engines and tail unit, a completely revised fuselage was necessary. Pan American was always interested in new ideas and in recognising the merits of the scheme provided the backing for three examples of the proposed Model 307. Further down the west coast of America, Douglas was already busy with the four-engined DC-4, but strangely it was destined to remain unpressurised which in the long term was to prove a costly mistake by the Californian company.

At last Boeing had reason to be optimistic about the prospects for its advanced transport which had been christened 'Stratoliner'. Its completely circular fuselage had a diameter of 12ft thereby affording ample room for the 33 passengers. As an alternative the 307 was equipped with 16 bunks plus nine reclining seats, but whatever the configuration, the travellers experienced the high standard of comfort pioneered by Boeing years before. TWA was an early customer bringing the total ordered to nine, but with World War 2 imminent, the manufacturer was fully committed to the production of B-17s so further work on the 307 was prematurely abandoned with only 10 examples built. Impressed into military service, the Stratoliners proved to be extremely reliable and sufficiently durable to return to civilian hands in 1945.

As the 307 was shelved, so work began on a pressurised long range bomber. As usual the Model 345 included innovations well ahead of its time and took Boeing into areas not hitherto penetrated. First flown in September 1942, after an early history of fires largely due to taking the engine to its performance limit, the initial batch of B-29s entered service in the late spring of 1944 to take part in the Far Eastern campaign. Although production ended shortly after the war, the type remained in service for some years in various guises. In addition the later B-50 was developed in the late 1940s and was destined to become the last piston-engined aircraft built for the USAF.

History has a habit of repeating itself and sure enough the immediate postwar period found the aircraft manufacturers suddenly deprived of work due to the drastic cutbacks on contracts for military aircraft. Boeing was no exception but of course had experienced such events 25 years earlier. A return to the commercial scene was the answer but both Douglas and Lockheed had a considerable start in this field. During the war Boeing had developed the Model 367 transport for the air force as the C-97. There was a close relationship to both the B-29 and B-50, but as in the B-17/Stratoliner case, the fuselage was an original design. It therefore seemed logical to update the machine for sale to the airlines. Unable to await sufficient orders before launching the aircraft, Boeing began work, acutely conscious of the $1 million cost of each example.

A financial crisis was averted on 28 November 1945 when Pan American expressed its support by ordering 20 Stratocruisers, by which name the Model 377 was now known. At the time it was the largest contract ever placed for a commercial machine and certainly paved the way for more carriers to follow suit. Another 18 months or so passed before the prototype flew, followed by a similar period until the first was delivered to Pan American in January 1949. It became a very popular transport while in service, its ample proportions permitting a two-deck layout connected by means of a spiral staircase. For the first time the space allowed passengers to wander

around during the course of the flight, a practice nowadays rife in both narrow and wide-bodied aircraft. Standard versions normally carried 75 seats of which 56 could be turned into berths since this was still a time when sleep was considered best accomplished in a horizontal mode. On higher density sorties such luxuries were eliminated so that 114 seats could be installed.

When the last of the 56 Stratocruisers to be built was delivered to BOAC as G-AKGM on 24 March 1950, the Comet had already become the world's first jet-powered airliner. Although the piston-engined types were in wide-scale use until the end of the 1950s, Boeing realised that there had to be no delay in tackling this new challenge if its commercial division was to remain in business.

Below:
The bulk of the postwar Stratocruiser is apparent in this shot of BOAC's G-ANTZ in 1955. Although relatively few of the airliners were sold, its military counterpart operated in large numbers with the USAF as the C-97 and KC-97. *G. W. Pennick*

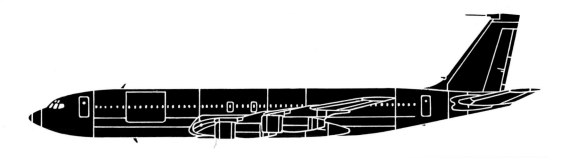

Enter the Jet

While Boeing had considered a jet-engined bomber in the mid-war years, the result of the deliberations generally centred around a B-29 suitably adapted to take a pair of turbojets under each wing. German designers on the other hand had progressed much further to accumulate considerable detailed knowledge of swept wings and the new form of propulsion. After the war had ended this information was acquired by those astute enough to recognise its value with the result that Boeing was one of the companies that benefited by the windfall. Following detailed analysis of the liberated findings and discussions with German scientists, the existing straight-wing project was abandoned in favour of the Model 448, a four-jet machine with a 35° swept wing. At an early stage it became apparent that there would be insufficient power available, so two more engines were mounted in pods outboard of the two pairs already slung under the wings.

Traditionally following Boeing's Strato theme for names, the newcomer was allocated Stratojet and with the mock-up complete, the air force authorities were invited to consider the project in April 1946. Subject to a few detailed changes, the go-ahead was given for the company to build two prototypes of what had now become the Model 450 or XB-47. In a remarkably short time considering the extent of the new technology involved, the first machine (46-065) was proudly rolled out at Seattle in September 1947, the forerunner of over 2,000 to be built by Boeing and its sub-contractors, Douglas and Lockheed. Three months later the aircraft made its maiden flight without incident on 17 December, an occasion followed by a lengthy test programme. Both prototypes were fitted with General Electric J-35 engines, but during 1949 these were exchanged for J-47s which produced a thrust of 5,200lb compared with the original power plant's 4,000lb. Following further tests it was 1 March 1950 before the first production B-47A was completed and deliveries could begin.

Because of the thin wing, a new location had to be found for the undercarriage. A novel solution was chosen which positioned the two pairs of main

Below:
Landing the B-47 was quite an interesting experience which certainly would not have appealed to fare-paying passengers. In this view the position of the well-spaced engine pods can be seen. *Boeing*

wheels in tandem formation under the fuselage, with stability on the ground maintained by means of a retractable outrigger below the two inboard engine pods. Another characteristic of the B-47 was its high landing speed which had an adverse effect upon brakes when attempting to remain within the airfield boundary once on the ground. To assist in achieving this reasonable objective the machine was equipped with a tail parachute which was deployed as the wheels made contact with the runway.

Originally devised as a high-altitude medium bomber, as the years progressed and ground-to-air missiles became a reality, it was no longer prudent to consider jaunts over Russian territory. New tactics were therefore necessary and these demanded that the B-47s were operated at very low levels to avoid detection. Although resembling a large fighter in appearance, there the comparison ended. It was just not built to withstand the pressures resulting from the violent gyrations it was now expected to endure. Hence it was not long before a series of crashes due to structural failure hastened the end of the B-47's operational life, although it was the mid-1960s before the last was withdrawn. During its career it had been the mainstay of the US Strategic Air Force (SAC) and set a number of speed records including the American coast-to-coast and the transatlantic. A B-47 also made history by becoming the first jet type to overfly the North Pole in September 1951.

Above:
Experience gained with the Stratojet was valuable during the evolution of the Dash Eighty. This particular example is 31843, a B-47E operated by the 307th Bomb Wing based at Lincoln AFB, Nb was at O'Hare Airport, Chicago, in May 1961.
Stevens/G. W. Pennick

Right:
These two view of the B-52 clearly show the undercarriage and engine arrangement subsequently rejected during the design stage of the civil airliner. Climbing away is 61-0027 of the 17th Bomb Wing based at Wright Patterson AFB, while the 28th Bomb Wing's 60-0037 is on its landing run. *P. Bennett/G. W. Pennick*

Thanks to the considerable postwar sales of the B-47 and B-50, Boeing was financially secure by the early 1950s and the nation's leading aircraft manufacturer. It had already been entrusted with the latest air force project after competing with other companies during the 1940s. At first turboprops were specified for the proposed large heavy bomber despite the success of the jet-powered B-47. Gradually the B-52 evolved to finally be accepted with eight turbojets mounted in pairs and overall bearing a marked similarity to its immediate forebear. This changed to some extent with production models because the B-47-style cockpit design was abandoned in favour of a normal flight deck arrangement. Its sheer size posed problems of their own necessitating larger buildings

to house the monster, while in the air its thirst had to be quenched if it was to be effective in its intended role.

Basic flight refuelling had been attempted by Boeing as early as 1929, and although reasonably successful, the method used was primitive in the extreme. With more pressing matters in hand the idea was quietly filed in the pending section rather than abandoned completely. Twenty years or so later Boeing was asked to carry out feasibility studies for refuelling B-29s in flight by using a similar type as a tanker. Subsequently a substantial number of the species were converted thereby guaranteeing them a useful new career. As a logical progression the C-97 was also offered as an airborne filling station. Designated KC-97, this tanker version was destined to become an important member of SAC. It had a distinct advantage over the B-29 because it could be readily transformed into a freighter or troop transport without the removal of the refuelling equipment. As B-47s replaced the B-50s in front-line service, so the latter were also converted into tankers. In this case the aircraft sprouted a pair of jet engines under the wings as encouragement to reach greater heights and travel faster.

While faithfully carrying out the duties for some years, the tankers really belonged to the propeller era. Mixing them with jets was not ideal and presented problems for the faster machines when trying to formate during the refuelling process. Boeing was well aware of these short-comings and applied itself to the task of building a turbojet tanker so that the recipients could maintain speed during the transfer of fuel thereby increasing their operational efficiency. At the same time the company also realised that it needed to be prepared to meet the forthcoming civil airliner requirement although there was still a certain reluctance to become involved at a too early stage.

In the UK there was no such feeling. In 1949 the Comet 1 had become the world's first commercial airliner to fly when it took off from Hatfield on 27 July. A circular fuselage was designed to carry 36 passengers and the moderately swept wing was of a sufficiently thick section to contain the four de Havilland Ghost turbojets near each root. An intensive period of test flying then began with the prototype which was joined in July 1950 by the second machine. Handed over to BOAC in April of the following year, the airline began a series of route proving expeditions to establish techniques for operating the new generation aircraft. Meanwhile production of the Comet was proceeding apace to enable the first (G-ALYP) to be delivered to the proud owner on 8 April 1952. From January regular simulated schedules had been flown between Johannesburg and Heathrow, but on 2 May 1952 history was made when the world's first

fare paying passengers on a jet airliner left London for South Africa. By October BOAC had 10 Comets on strength and was busily expanding its route network to include the 10,200-mile trek to Tokyo.

In America the success of the Comet was viewed with concern especially since it was achieving 89% load factors and cutting flying times by half on some sectors. Nonetheless the airliners and the travelling public were happy with piston engines for the time being to such a degree that new models continued to be introduced despite the threat of the jet. Types such as the DC-6, DC-7 and the Super Constellation appeared, while Boeing's contribution was of course the Stratocruiser, but compared with the others it did not fare very well in terms of sales.

Although contributing its full share of pessimistic observations about the economics of turbojet transport operation, in April 1952 Boeing decided it was time to join the race. Already Douglas had announced its intention to offer the DC-8 to the airlines and had already invited potential customers to Santa Monica to inspect a full-scale mock-up of the project. Estimates placed its speed at about 560mph and the company was confident that it would be able to meet its target for getting the new airliner into service in 1958. At this stage the Californian manufacturer was considered the leader in the field just as it had previously been in the piston-engined market. Principally this was due to the company's resolve to finance the development from its own resources, unlike Boeing which was aiming to secure government contracts for a military variant before embarking on its civil counterpart.

Unexpectedly Douglas suspended work on the DC-8 in 1953 to concentrate on the DC-7. In the short term this aircraft certainly helped the manufacturer to maintain its dominant position. Even in 1957 deliveries totalled 123 and to this figure could be added 44 DC-6s, but this supremacy could not last because the Boeing jet was poised for its service entry in 1958. Sure enough the only representative of the piston-engined airliner era to leave the Douglas facility during the year was a single DC-6, although the company did also manage to produce 21 of its four-jet DC-8. A belated decision to resume work on the type had made this possible, but in the meantime Boeing had used the opportunity to good effect and was now well in the lead.

Unfortunately, in Europe the Comet 1 had met with a series of disasters which led to the grounding of all surviving specimens in 1954. Eventually the cause of the tragedies proved to have been metal fatigue brought about by the continual cycles of cabin pressurisation. Once this was understood, remedial action was possible in subsequent models, but the damage had been done to the reputation of the aircraft and the market advantage lost. Boeing was once again the main beneficiary of the setback.

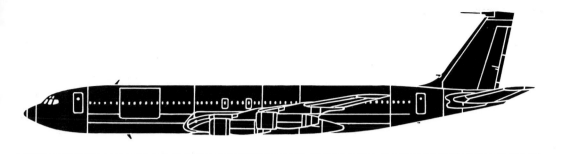

Some Boeing Milestones

Model	Number built	Remarks
B&W 1	2	Two-seat, twin-float biplane
C	58	Two-seat, twin-float biplane
40	86	Boeing's first multi-passenger transport
80	16	A tri-motor accommodating 12 passengers
200/221	2	An advanced monoplane mail and passenger carrier
246	5	Twin-engined monoplane bomber
247	75	Twin-engined monoplane airliner accommodating 10 passengers
294	1	Experimental four-engined heavy bomber (XB-15)
299	12,731	Became B-17 with the USAAF
307	10	33-seat pressurised airliner known as the Stratoliner
314	12	Long range, four-engined flying boat accommodating up to 74 passengers
345	3,974 (B-29), 347 (B-50)	Pressurised heavy bomber introduced during World War 2 and later for use in other roles. Updated version was B-50
367	77 C-97, 808 KC-97	Used as a large capacity transport but primarily as a tanker
367–80	1	Prototype for the KC-135 tanker and variants plus the 707 airliner
377	56	Civil postwar development of the C-97 and used for long range services with between 50 and 100 passengers according to type of route
450	2,040	Six-engined medium range bomber for the USAF (B-47)
464	744	Eight-engined heavy bomber for USAF (B-52)
707	813	Jet airliner produced in a number of versions. Total does not include later E-3 airframes
717	820	Introduced as the KC-135 tanker and developed into several other versions
720	154	Smaller capacity airliner originally known as the 707-020

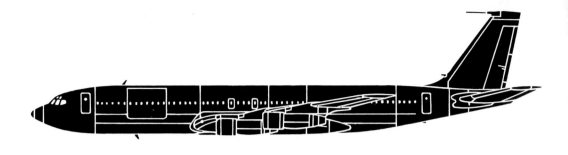

707 Development

Bearing in mind the earlier B-17/Stratoliner and B-29/Stratocruiser relationships, it was perhaps not surprising that the first outline sketches used the Model 367 (KC-97) as the basis for the new jet-powered machine. One of the breed was so converted to see if it was a practical proposition to re-engine the fleet, but despite a distinctly improved performance, somehow the bulbous shape did not really lend itself to such a radical update. Back at the drawing boards the next logical step was to use the B-47 expertise, a well-proven design by this time. In an attempt to confuse the competition Boeing continued to refer to the new project as the Model 367 throughout its early days. A great number of different layouts were suggested, each being allocated a suffix number for identification purposes.

Consequently there was little information forthcoming, but despite the secrecy surrounding the Boeing activities, it gradually became known that whatever was eventually rolled-out of the factory would officially be known as the Model 367-80, later to be universally known as the Dash Eighty. More details were released during the course of 1953 and for the first time the designation 707 was used, albeit incorrectly as later events revealed because this identity was reserved for the true civil airliner still to emerge. Although the venture was initially funded by the company to the tune of some $16 million, there was general belief that the US Government had given its moral backing so there was every expectation that the USAF would confirm it with an order. With this in mind it was the tanker version that took priority in the early stages so that if the so-called gamble succeeded then the development costs of the future airliner derivative would be considerably reduced.

From the very beginning the fundamental consideration in the design of the new machine had been to reduce operating costs in all ways possible. While the size and speed had an important bearing on the seat-mile figures, time-consuming engineering maintenance effort could offset this advantage unless steps were taken to ensure ease of access. Every opportunity was taken to simplify procedures whether it was a minor detail or a major task involving an engine change. For the latter operation a system of colour coding at disconnect points was devised as an aid to greater efficiency, but everything played its part in keeping out-of-service times to a minimum. Experience with the J-47 turbojet in military service showed that the overhaul period was now 1,750hr which was likely to be extended to 2,000hr for new commercial jets. This was a considerable improvement on the piston engines while the number of in-flight shut-downs reported also compared favourably with the older technology.

Thought was also given to the co-ordination of life-expired component renewals so that these could all be changed during the programmed routine overhauls rather than outside these periods. In an effort to reduce turn-round times the cargo holds were given three doors and a loading system developed. Refuelling processes were speeded up by providing four under-wing pressure points which permitted fuel to be supplied at 1,500gal/min.

Although adopting the B-47/B-52 style of wing with a 35° sweep back, it was intended that the transport would possess only four engines. At first these were mounted in two pairs under each wing, but ultimately single pods were chosen for the Pratt & Whitney JT3s, the civil equivalent of the J-57s installed in the B-52. Not only did this formation give a better weight distribution for the structure, but also the accessibility for maintenance was greatly improved especially since hinged panels were liberally provided. There was also the all-important safety aspect to consider. Already firmly believing in hanging the engines beneath the wings rather than burying them within, Boeing thought that under certain circumstances any problem with one of a pair might necessitate the shut-down of its partner thereby reducing the available power by half.

Another feature of the B-47 that would be decidedly unusual for an airliner was the undercarriage arrangement. Drooping wings supported by little outriggers plus the four main wheels in tandem formation under the fuselage would be viewed with considerable apprehension by the average traveller. Accordingly a completely new tricycle layout was adopted with the main legs retracting sideways so that each of the two four-wheeled bogies were housed within the lower fuselage. The latter still retained the 'double-bubble' cross section common to the C-97 series, but the familiar crease along the side had been smoothed out for the new jet. Two large cargo doors were fitted fore and aft, the latter being deleted from the aircraft eventually adopted by the USAF.

After two years' work, the hangar doors at Renton were opened on 14 May 1954 and the Dash Eighty was rolled out with due pomp and ceremony before thousands of employees and guests. Finished in a somewhat bilious hue of yellow and brown, the creation certainly did not

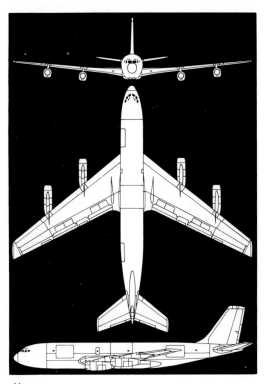

Above:
The Dash Eighty in its original form.

Below:
Roll-out of the Dash Eighty in May 1954.
Boeing Archives

resemble a Model 367. Neither, for that matter, did it look very much like an airliner; its almost windowless body underlined its intended military role. Nevertheless it did carry the appropriate civil registration, N70700.

Taxying trials began almost immediately but on 22 May the Dash Eighty disgraced itself by suffering the collapse of its port undercarriage leg. Structural damage was slight although the mishap put the programme back some six weeks while repairs were effected. These completed, the delayed maiden flight of America's first jet-powered transport took place on 15 July in the hands of Mr A. M. (Tex) Johnston, Boeing's chief test pilot, the uneventful sortie lasting 1hr 24min. As is usual on these occasions the time was spent in general handling trials at medium and approach speeds. Although the Dash Eighty had taken off from its birthplace at Renton, the landing was made at Boeing Field, Seattle, the site for the subsequent test work.

After a two-day break the programme restarted, thereafter proceeding very rapidly so that during the eight days following the first trip aloft, a total flying time of 15hr 46min was logged which included both high-altitude and high-speed excursions. For instance, on 19 July the aircraft was taken to 42,000ft and checks were made at speeds exceeding Mach 0.8 during a flight lasting 2hr 19min. Two sorties amounting to 2hr 10min were made on the next day, these being used to cover functional checks of the systems, but the longest mission to date was made on 21 July. During a 3hr 55min absence from base the prototype was taken to its operating cruise altitude whereupon the engine cooling data was examined. Restarts were tried and fast descents employing airbrakes were made to verify the tank venting arrangements. Even during this early series of tests the aircraft's pressurisation and ventilation system was in full use. All of the outings were in the charge of Tex Johnston with R. L. Loesch acting as co-pilot, the pair being joined after the third expedition by engineers and observers.

It was at this stage and well before any conclusive proof that the type would indeed be suitable for use as a tanker, that the USAF decided to award a contract to Boeing for 29 of its Model 717 aircraft to be designated KC-135. It was a welcome boost for the company's morale at a time when there had been little positive response from the airlines about the civil variant. As if to attract some attention, the prototype itself made the headlines when it ran off the hard strip while landing after a test flight on 5 August. Brake failure caused the machine to come to rest in a sandy area alongside the runway, but fortunately there were no injuries and only superficial damage to the airframe.

Apart from this relatively minor event, the first section of the programme was completed on 2 October without incident. Fifty hours had been allocated for the purpose, but in the event only 43hr 27min were needed, the final 26hr 37min being spread over only nine days. Included in this last phase was the longest trip embarked upon to date which consumed 5hr 5min. With little to hinder the start of stage two, flying continued until the end of the year when Boeing was able to report that the prototype had now flown 92hr 30min in total since it first left the ground on 15 July. Cruising at altitudes higher than the previously announced 42,000ft, the aircraft had also been flown uneventfully at speeds exceeding the forecast 550mph.

Since additional instrumentation had to be fitted prior to the beginning of the next round of trials, the opportunity was taken to perform the routine 100hr inspection of the engines. None of the four JT3s had given any trouble during the entire programme, so the checks were able to be made without disturbing them in their pods. Such was the confidence in the Dash Eighty that during a two-month period when Boeing Field's main 10,000ft runway was undergoing repairs, the prototype regularly operated from a 5,800ft taxiway without problem. For much of the time the two company employees shared the workload on the flight deck, but there was now a third person qualified as a captain on the type because the resident Air Research & Development Command test pilot, Lt-Col G. M. Townsend, had also been checked out.

Naturally if the machine was to fulfil its promise as a tanker, then a dispensing device was needed. As soon as the main flying characteristics had been satisfactorily explored, the Dash Eighty was equipped with a Boeing-designed boom on the underside of the rear fuselage. Despite this further indication of its future military role, the Dash Eighty was also used for sales demonstrations to airline representatives. Commercial pilots from Pan American, American Airlines and United Air Lines were amongst those given the opportunity to handle the prototype.

As a logical extension of this marketing effort Boeing despatched the Dash Eighty on a transcontinental journey to give interested customers an idea of the possible capabilities of the future civil transport version. Flying from Seattle to Washington DC, the aircraft managed to complete the outbound sector in 3hr 58min, maintaining an average speed of 592mph for the 2,340 miles. After a 3hr turn round the return trip was accomplished in 4hr 8min at the slightly lower average speed of 567mph. For the exercise the prototype operated from Larson AFB, Moses Lake, flying over Seattle for timing purposes before climbing on course to the east coast. A similar procedure was carried out as it overflew Washington before landing at Andrews AFB, some nine miles east of the capital.

All this effort proved worthwhile because Boeing was at last rewarded with an order for the Model 707 airliner. Pan American had long been interested in the new generation jet airliner projects of both Boeing and Douglas, the latter by this time having resumed its work on the DC-8. Both types had their merits so it was extremely difficult to decide which aircraft to select at this early stage. In the case of the first 707s, range restrictions would make transatlantic operations difficult whereas its rival was powered by JT4A engines which made it more suitable for the long overwater sectors. On the other hand Boeing was able to promise a much earlier delivery date. Pan American hesitated for a time but in due course ordered 25 DC-8s backed up as an insurance measure by 20 707s on 13 October 1955. Deliveries were expected in December 1958 and the aircraft were intended to carry 104 passengers when a first class section was provided or 125 when configured for all-tourist work. While the order was not unexpected, the size of the commitment certainly raised a few eyebrows.

Work had of course been proceeding with the development of the KC-135, the first of which (55-3118) was rolled out on 18 July 1956. Organised to squeeze the maximum publicity benefits, the occasion was contrived to coincide with the roll-out of the last KC-97 (53-3616) off the production line. Overhead the Dash Eighty and a B-52 paid their respects to both old and new as they stood together in the sun. Showmanship indeed. Yet had the affair been postponed for three days, Boeing's 40th anniversary could have been celebrated at the same time. Perhaps it was thought that it would have overshadowed the fact that some 21 months after the KC-135 was ordered, the aircraft was a reality and ready for its maiden flight.

This took place on 31 August 1956 when the machine left Renton for Boeing Field. After several more excursions, the KC-135 was given additional equipment before embarking on a programme which included the first in-flight transfer of fuel, the receiver being a B-52. Thereafter the trials continued smoothly allowing deliveries of the species to the USAF to begin in mid-1957, thereby marking the start of a successful career of indefinite length.

Boeing had not been overjoyed when it virtually became the second choice of Pan American, but

any disappointment was short-lived. Swiftly a whole family of airliners was on offer, designed to meet all the varying requirements of the airlines. Anxious not to be left behind, teams from carriers around the world arrived at the Boeing and Douglas plants to see for themselves before embarking on a major spending spree.

There was not long to wait before the next orders were received by the Seattle company. American Airlines proved to be the first of the second wave by ordering an impressive 30 machines for its domestic network. Continental also planned this role for four 707s while Braniff favoured five examples of a more powerful version identified as the Model 220. This was deemed suitable for operations in the hot South American climate where many of the airports are situated at high altitudes. With this degree of interest at such an early stage, Boeing embarked upon the task of producing the new airliner within the promised timescale which was aimed at a service entry date in late 1958.

At first this could seem rather protracted bearing in mind the experience already gained with the Dash Eighty and the fact that the KC-135 was in service by June 1957. However, while looking alike, the 707 was by no means a civil version of its military relative. This applied particularly to the fuselage which had a greater diameter and possessed a completely different cross-section to that of the KC-135. At the time it was the largest passenger cabin to have been built, its length of over 100ft (30.48m) producing an air of spaciousness never before experienced. A vast number of rectangular windows along each side helped in this respect and it meant that in normal circumstances passengers had at least two through which to peer at the outside world. Dimensionally they were quite small, measuring only some 9in×12in, an element of caution being exercised by the designers in the light of the early Comet structural failures. Apart from this factor, it was also considered that the size allowed a greater flexibility for the interior layout. Whatever the reason for rejecting the use of large elliptical windows, there is little doubt that the latter enjoy greater passenger appeal.

Built in four sections, the first portion of fuselage extended from the nose back to the forward entrance door, the second stretched from this point to the trailing edge of the wing, with section three continuing to the rear pressure bulkhead. All that remained made up the fourth segment. Two main spars joined to a fuselage-width centre section provided the basis for the wing structure within which most of the space was taken up by fuel tanks.

While the tail control surfaces were of a conventional design, those located on the wing introduced many unusual features. Two sets of ailerons were provided; one in the traditional spot towards the wing tips, the other at mid-span. Used exclusively at low speeds, the former were only operative when the flaps were lowered, at other times remaining locked in the neutral position. On the other hand the inboard ailerons had a short span and wide chord and were used at all times. Their location divided the trailing edge main flaps which when extended by 9° or more, also activated a small leading edge flap situated just inboard of the outer engine pod. This device was added at a late stage in the 707s development and was designed to improve control at low speeds when taking off with the wing at a high angle of attack. Spoilers were located on the upper surface of the wing immediately in front of the flaps, their purpose being to improve manoeuvrability during the approach stages, particularly in crosswinds. For the curious traveller in the cabin, the constant movement of portions of the wing proved fascinating if not alarming, especially during the preparations for landing. Nowadays the practice is commonplace.

No time was lost in establishing a production line at Renton so that by mid-1957 the first of the 707s was easily recognisable. Such was the progress that Boeing was able to roll out the aircraft on 28 October for preflight tests to take place before its maiden sortie on 20 December. This was several days ahead of schedule, but unlike other inaugural ventures into the sky, it was merely a 7min ferry trip to Boeing Field. Painted in company colours, it was retained for the duration of the trials before becoming a member of Pan American's fleet as N708PA almost one year later. This specimen then became the last of the airline's batch of six Series 120s to be delivered, the original order that helped launch the 707 having subsequently been amended to a new total of 23 aircraft, but specifying that 17 would be the longer range Series 320.

By May two more Series 120s (N707PA and N709PA) had become involved in the certification programme, the former operating from Edwards AFB for take-off and landing trials painted in full Pan American livery. Still well ahead of its planned timetable, Boeing set a revised target of 18 July as the date when test flying would end. This achieved, the company then had to await the completion of the not inconsiderable amount of paperwork by the authorities before a provisional certificate was issued on 15 August 1958. As a result the 707 was permitted to be used for training purposes, route-proving or non-revenue trips by airlines. There was an exception to the latter stipulation because Pan American was duly authorised to operate commercial cargo flights between New York and San Juan, Puerto Rico.

No time was lost. Delivery of N709PA to the airline was made on the same day so that a three-week period of familiarisation training for the selected crews could begin. On 23 August history was made when the aircraft became the first American civil turbojet transport to operate a commercial service. Since it carried a consignment of freight to Puerto Rico on the outbound sector, a similar opportunity existed for another noteworthy statistic to be recorded during the return leg on the following day. This time its claim to fame came with

Below:
One of Pan American's early Series 121s, N707PA was later modified to 'B' standard in 1964.

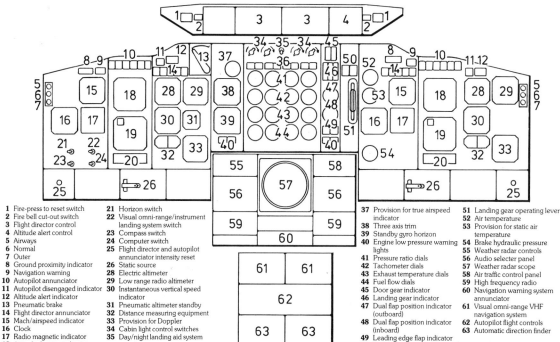

1 Fire-press to reset switch	**21** Horizon switch
2 Fire bell cut-out switch	**22** Visual omni-range/instrument
3 Flight director control	landing system switch
4 Altitude alert control	**23** Compass switch
5 Airways	**24** Computer switch
6 Normal	**25** Flight director and autopilot
7 Outer	annunciator intensity reset
8 Ground proximity indicator	**26** Static source
9 Navigation warning	**28** Electric altimeter
10 Autopilot annunciator	**29** Low range radio altimeter
11 Autopilot disengaged indicator	**30** Instantaneous vertical speed
12 Altitude alert indicator	indicator
13 Pneumatic brake	**31** Pneumatic altimeter standby
14 Flight director annunciator	**32** Distance measuring equipment
15 Mach/airspeed indicator	**33** Provision for Doppler
16 Clock	**34** Cabin light control switches
17 Radio magnetic indicator	**35** Day/night landing aid system
18 Attitude director indicator	warning
19 Horizontal situation indicator	**36** Cabin light control
20 Space for landing aid system	

37 Provision for true airspeed	**51** Landing gear operating lever
indicator	**52** Air temperature
38 Three axis trim	**53** Provision for static air
39 Standby gyro horizon	temperature
40 Engine low pressure warning	**54** Brake hydraulic pressure
lights	**55** Weather radar controls
41 Pressure ratio dials	**56** Audio selecter panel
42 Tachometer dials	**57** Weather radar scope
43 Exhaust temperature dials	**58** Air traffic control panel
44 Fuel flow dials	**59** High frequency radio
45 Door gear indicator	**60** Navigation warning system
46 Landing gear indicator	annunciator
47 Dual flap position indicator	**61** Visual omni-range VHF
(outboard)	navigation system
48 Dual flap position indicator	**62** Autopilot flight controls
(inboard)	**63** Automatic direction finder
49 Leading edge flap indicator	
50 Rudder boost control/esential	
power control	

its arrival at Idlewild, New York, thereby becoming the first jet-powered airliner engaged in a revenue-earning flight to land in the US.

Needless to say one of Pan American's main ambitions was to introduce the 707 on to the prestigious New York-London route as quickly as possible, so Heathrow was therefore an early target during the spate of proving excursions. For many it meant an early start on Monday 8 September because N709PA was due to arrive at about 08.00. In the event it was 08.02 when it touched down on runway 28L after its transatlantic crossing via Gander, Newfoundland, and Shannon. Basically a training mission for the flight crews, it was also used to give the ground support teams experience in handling the new machine. This applied particularly at the transit stops where visits would be more infrequent than at the main terminals. Its arrival and departure also afforded the opportunity for some noise measurements to allay or confirm the fears of those likely to be affected by the forthcoming regular appearances.

Already 130 hours had been accumulated by N709PA since joining Pan American in August and it was flown at the maximum weight of 190,000lb agreed for the duration of the provisional certificate. On the flight deck there were positions for five crew members, one being a jump-seat for training purposes. In addition to the normal two pilots and engineer, a navigator was also intended to be on board for the transatlantic services. Despite the airline's keenness to put the type on the route, only the Series 120s were available and these were really not intended for such long stages. As hoped, after 700 hours of flying by the three production machines, the full certificate was awarded on 23 September to remove the last hurdle preventing regular commercial operations. Having served its purpose well, N709PA was returned to the manufacturer for refurbishing to airline standard while in exchange Boeing delivered N710PA on 20 September and N711PA on 17 October, both of which were in a fully certificated state.

Meanwhile in the UK there was every hope that BOAC would be able to inaugurate its own jet services at an early date. Thousands of hours had been flown by the Comet Mk 2E and Mk 3 during

Left:
When the 707 first entered service the flight deck often carried a navigator in addition to the two pilots and engineer. There is also another seat for a supplementary crew member behind the left hand pilot.

Below left:
707 instrument panel.

Below:
Flight deck layout.

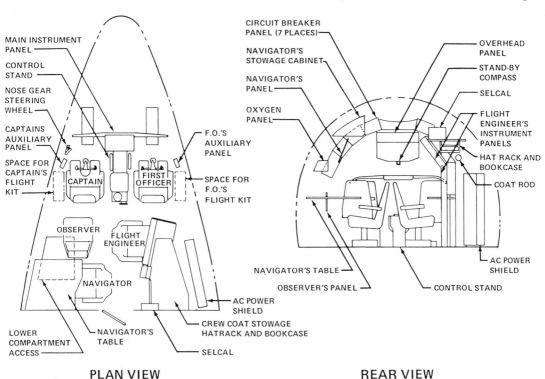

PLAN VIEW   REAR VIEW

the course of training and proving flights, so all that was needed was the type certificate for the Mk 4 and this was forthcoming on 30 September. With remarkable speed which was completely out of character, the airline made plans to operate its two newly delivered Comets across the Atlantic before the American carrier. Enterprisingly the route was inaugurated in both directions on 4 October, G-APDB having previously positioned to Idlewild. It made the eastbound crossing non-stop aided by a favourable wind, but its colleague (G-APDC) had a 1hr refuelling stop at Gander, which was to be the normal practice for flights heading for the US. Thereafter the frequencies built up as more aircraft were delivered by de Havilland until during December it was possible to maintain a daily rotation.

It was a fine achievement especially since the launch came a month earlier than anticipated. Undoubtedly it stole some of Pan American's glory because another three weeks passed before the US carrier began transatlantic schedules with N711PA on 26 October. First to benefit was the New York-Paris route which was served on a daily basis despite the availability of only two 707s. Proving flights continued to London in the meantime culminating in a daily schedule to and from New York commencing on 16 November. Although the situation was eased to some extent with the redelivery of N709PA after modifications, the machines quickly proved their ability to withstand the pressures of high utilisation.

Like the Comet, range restrictions prevented the westbound 707s making the crossing non-stop under normal conditions. This meant that either Gander or Keflavik, Iceland, were used for refuelling, although occasionally flights in the other direction found it necesary to make a precautionary call at Shannon if the usually helpful winds were less than favourable. On average the journey times between London and New York were 8hr 45min and 6hr 35min when eastbound.

At the outset the Series 120s were configured with 40 first class seats arranged in pairs either side of the centre aisle, while in the rear economy standard cabin another 66 were installed in a six-abreast formation. Between the flight deck and front compartment there was a lounge provided on the port side which could if necessary be used by fare-paying passengers. It was still early days and the idea that comfort was essential had overflowed from the piston era.

By using the doors at both ends of the cabin, travellers were able to board and disembark fairly quickly, but quite soon it became apparent that it was necessary for airports to realise that there had to be a revision in procedures as more and more of the new airliners entered service. Additional check-in facilities were required while baggage

handling and immigration could cause considerable delays for arriving passengers with the resultant congestion. As an indication of the growing popularity of the new mode of travel, in barely two months from start-up until the end of 1958, Pan American had carried 19,557 passengers on the New York to Paris and London routes. Over roughly the same period 3,913 people chose to use the smaller capacity Comet 4s operated by BOAC with a first class layout.

At the beginning of December, Pan American had received five 707s from Boeing which were sufficient for its current needs. In fact it was able to wet lease two aircraft to National Airlines so that the latter could introduce the type to the lucrative New York-Miami route commencing on 10 December. Always a busy sector, the enterprise was rewarded with high load factors as the Americans sampled this latest form of transport to the winter sun.

As the second customer for the 707 back in 1955, American Airlines was naturally next to receive its allocation. Rolled out as early as 1 July 1958, the first (N7501A) was not delivered until 23 October and then only with a provisional certificate to enable the airline to begin training. At the end of the year the fleet began to assemble so that American could realistically plan its first schedule for 25 January. On this date, with two 707s available, the carrier introduced the type to transcontinental work on the New York-Los Angeles route. During the next 18 days 3,720 passengers flew on the service representing a load factor of 99.5%! Of course much was due to the novelty value but at least the domestic jets had arrived. Trans World was one of American's competitors on the west coast routes and although it had temporary possession of a 707 in early 1959, it was 17 March before the company finally took delivery of its first (N732TW) for operational service. Only three days later TWA slotted this single machine into its New York-San Francisco schedules with great success, a process repeated on the Los Angeles run after the second 707 was received from Seattle on 30 March.

Until now only the Series 120 had been employed, but the time was rapidly approaching when other models would be available. One of the family announced by Boeing at the beginning of the 707's life was the Series 320 Intercontinental version which was destined to prove very popular with the airlines. Both Air France and Sabena chose the variant during December 1955, but only shortly

Above right:
A general view of the 707 production line when at its peak. *Boeing Archives*

Right:
By 1960 production of the 707 was well under way at Seattle. *Boeing*

before Pan American realised the wisdom in reducing its existing Series 120 order in favour of the long range specimen. As a result the first 12 airframes off the production line were -120s, deliveries being split equally between the two launch customers, but the 13th became the initial -320 for the US carrier. Rolled out at Renton in November 1958, it first ventured aloft on 11 January 1959 carrying the registration N714PA.

On board was a profusion of automatic equipment for recording every conceivable item of information about the machine's performance characteristics.If required this could be relayed to a ground station in advance of the aircraft landing with the wealth of data thereby saving time if not paper. Certification trials for the FAA began on 15 February, only 35 days after the first flight. By this time two -320s were flying and had already amassed 100 hours in the air. One of the pair devoted its time to proving its functional reliability while simulating airline operations. Several long distance flights were undertaken including a non-stop trip to Rome on 29 May, the 5,832 miles covered being the furthest attempted by a jet airliner at the time. Following a Great Circle course, the 707 overflew Keflavik, Glasgow and Zurich in a time of 11hr 6min. For most of the journey the aircraft cruised at Mach 0.78 reaching a maximum altitude of 39,160ft. Little time was spent in Italy because on the 30th it visited Paris, Brussels and Frankfurt before landing at Heathrow for a night stop. On the next day the -320 left for Seattle which was reached 9hr 36min later after an uneventful direct flight.

The purpose of the certification programme was to demonstrate to the FAA only those features which differed from the Series 120 rather than the complete aircraft. For this reason the forecast that the tests would not exceed six months was accurate because the new variant gained its type certificate on 15 July to pave the way for Pan American's first -320 (N715PA) to be delivered to the airline on 19 July. A second had arrived by 16 August, 10 days before the date chosen for the aircraft to enter service on the London-Los Angeles and San Francisco routes. On 10 October, after almost a year of excellent service by the -120s, Pan American was able to begin replacing them on the North Atlantic routes to London and Frankfurt.

In appearance there was little to indicate the difference between the two versions, although 8ft 5in (2.59m) had been added to the fuselage and there were proportionately more windows. In addition the wingspan had grown by 11ft 7in (3.51m) and the engines changed to the more powerful JT4A-11 of 17,500lb thrust. With its fuel capacity increased to 23,815gal, a range of almost 5,000 miles was possible with a full load of 189 passengers.

Long before it had flown the first transatlantic commercial jet services, BOAC realised that the Comet 4s and Britannias would not be suitable competition for the later 707s such as the Series 320. There was a grave risk that the British flag carrier would be left behind if it did not join the other nations in adding the type to its inventory. Such thoughts were not voiced in public during 1955, when it was being stated that the Corporation was satisfied that its fleet requirements for well into the 1960s were already met by the aircraft on order.

A year later the policy had changed. This time the government had agreed to the purchase of 707s since it was unlikely that there would be any suitable British type available in the required timescale. Although the airline had calculated that it had a need for 17 aircraft, the cautious civil servant advisors trimmed this to 15, each costing £44 million. Accordingly an order was placed with Boeing in October 1956, the 11th to be received by the company. At least the choice of Rolls-Royce Conway 508s by BOAC pacified to a small degree those opposing the decision.

Otherwise similar to the Series 320 Intercontinental, the new variant was known as the -420 and had previously been chosen by both Air India and Lufthansa. Developed concurrently with the other 707 models, the first example was rolled out on 12 March 1959 to make its first flight on 19 May carrying the Boeing registration N31241. There was every confidence that FAA certification would be forthcoming late in the year to permit deliveries to BOAC to begin in December. Due to unforeseen delays this timetable was not followed with the result that the first aircraft (G-APFD) was not delivered until 28 April 1960.

To meet the British Air Registration Board's (ARB) conditions, a series of modifications had to be incorporated. Characteristics shown during recovery from an engine-out situation at low speeds had caused some concern so the new features were designed to reduce the risk of accidents in such an event. A fully power-assisted rudder system was requested for the -420 which replaced the standard method where the application of power depended upon the amount of rudder deflection applied. To further increase the stability of the 707 a 35in vertical fin extension and a new ventral fin was stipulated, which was also intended to act as a bumper to limit the angle of rotation at take-off. Tests of the latter were carried out at Edwards AFB

With the work completed, the -420 received its British Type Certificate from the ARB on 27 April 1960, but the four months' delay had proved costly for BOAC. As contracted the first machine should have been with the airline by the last day of December with the second following its example in February. From this point one was due each month until October when the flow was doubled until the final arrival in December. Start-up on the North Atlantic routes would then have been possible in mid-April with frequencies building up as the peak season approached. Unfortunately there was no other option but to scrap this plan in view of the lack of aircraft. It meant that for much of the year the Corporation's schedules had to remain in the hands of the Comets, Britannias and DC-7Cs, at a time when 12 of the 16 airlines flying to North America were offering non-stop jet services.

Above:
Early 707s were not fitted with the ventral fin under the rear fuselage, a modification which was discontinued when additional leading edge flaps were fitted to the later versions. *G. W. Pennick*

Right:
The JT3C turbojets which powered the first 707s were enclosed in a much smaller nacelle than those designed for the later variants. *G. W. Pennick*

using a metal strip supported on wooden blocks as a temporary measure. Results showed that the -420 would still become airborne even at an unrestricted angle, although the distance covered on the ground was unacceptable. Most of the changes were introduced by Boeing to subsequent aircraft on the line, but the ventral fin no longer proved necessary when additional leading edge flaps became a standard feature of the 320C series and a retrospective modification for the -320B.

Below right:
One of the BOAC batch of Conway-powered -436s, G-APFJ was delivered in September 1960. In 1977 it retired from scheduled work for a new life flying IT charters for British Airtours. Withdrawn in 1981, it is now to be found at the Cosford Aerospace Museum. *M. J. F. Bowyer*

Below:
Destined for Air India as VT-DSI, this 707-337B first flew in Boeing's company livery registered N68655.

178 TOURIST CLASS PASSENGERS

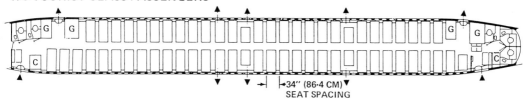

→| |← 34″ (86·4 CM)
SEAT SPACING

187 TOURIST CLASS PASSENGERS

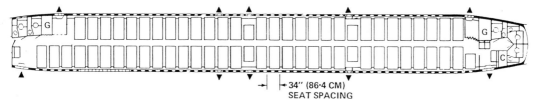

→| |← 34″ (86·4 CM)
SEAT SPACING

215 TOURIST CLASS PASSENGERS

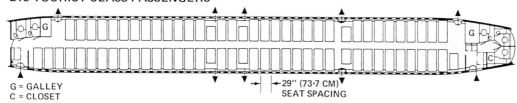

G = GALLEY
C = CLOSET

→| |← 29″ (73·7 CM)
SEAT SPACING

147 PASSENGERS

▲ 14 FIRST CLASS   133 TOURIST CLASS

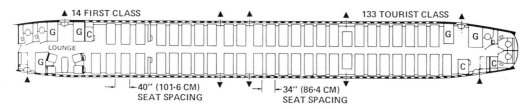

LOUNGE

|← 40″ (101·6 CM)
SEAT SPACING

→| |← 34″ (86·4 CM)
SEAT SPACING

152 PASSENGERS

▲ 16 FIRST CLASS   136 TOURIST CLASS

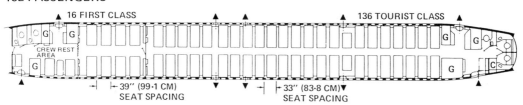

CREW REST AREA

|← 39″ (99·1 CM)
SEAT SPACING

→| |← 33″ (83·8 CM)
SEAT SPACING

157 PASSENGERS

▲ 16 FIRST CLASS   141 TOURIST CLASS

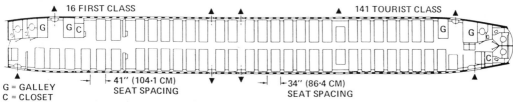

G = GALLEY
C = CLOSET

|← 41″ (104·1 CM)
SEAT SPACING

→| |← 34″ (86·4 CM)
SEAT SPACING

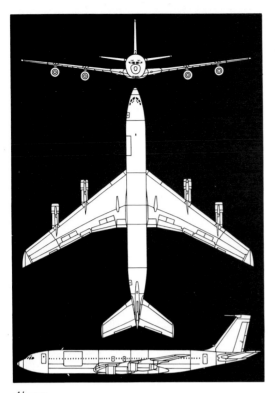

Above:
Three views of the 707-320C variant.

By early 1960 Intercontinental 707s had entered service on TWA's US coast-to-coast domestic schedules to give the carrier a speed advantage for the non-stop trip over its rivals, American and United. By mutual agreement all three had hitherto quoted identical journey times while using their JT3C-powered 707-120s and DC-8s, but with the availability of the -320 and the more powerful JT4A engines, the airline was able to offer a 15min reduction. United was due to take delivery of similarly powered DC-8s, but American had no such plans.

Observing the benefits in performance shown by the Conway turbofan engines, the company decided to order a variant known as the -120B to encourage the development of the Pratt & Whitney JT3D-1 turbofan producing 17,000lb thrust. This new type of engine was able to handle a greater volume of air through its large compressor stage, because instead of the entire output proceeding into the combustion chambers and turbine, a proportion was diverted around the engine. This brought a distinct increase in efficiency associated with reduced fuel consumption for longer range and lower costs.

Boeing gave the -120B additional leading edge flaps and the maximum take-off weight was increased to 258,000lb. The first example of this

variant (N7526A) was ready for roll-out on 13 May 1960 to be followed by its maiden flight on 22 June. Without waiting for the confirmation of the FAA's type approval, American decided to have all of its Series 120s brought up to the B standard. In November the first of 24 was returned to the manufacturer for the necessary changes, a task that took about five weeks or so to complete. By the end of January 1962 the fleet had been fully modernised and the airline had also taken delivery of the prototype.

A much improved Model 320 was launched in February 1961 when Pan American once again became the first customer for the new -320B. Also ordered by Air France and TWA, the latest Boeing offering had a range of 6,000 miles to outstrip the other commercial jets. Such an increase was made possible by the provision of JT3D-3 turbofans which produced 18,000lb thrust. Other improvements included full span leading edge flaps arranged to give a slotted effect, while those on the trailing edge received an additional section at the wing roots. New tips extended the overall span slightly, but the main benefit derived from this modification was the decreased drag. Seattle witnessed the latest 707's aerial baptism on 31 January 1962 and after a speedy test series, Pan American received all five of those ordered by mid-June. Generally they were reserved for the long non-stop sectors such as London-Los Angeles, which at 4,750 miles was well within the -320B's capabilities.

Noting the tend towards air cargo, Boeing produced a derivative for use in this role which became the -320C. It retained all of the advanced features of the B series, but in addition was fitted with a strengthened floor to withstand the heavier loads. On the forward port side of the fuselage an 11ft 2in × 7ft 7in (3.40m × 2.30m) door enabled pallets to be handled with ease into the cabin which was cleared to carry a 90,000lb payload, although in reality space restrictions tended to impose a limit of about 70,000lb. When operated as a combi, the freight was carried at the front, with the flight deck protected against accidents by a net stressed to 9g. Separated from this, the passengers in the rear compartment scarcely realised they were in half a freighter. In practice the -320Cs were normally configured either for carrying up to about 200 passengers or cargo work, the operators only taking advantage of the convertible feature to meet special demands. American Airlines became the first to order the variant as a dedicated freighter in 1962, a role portrayed by the lack of windows in the cabin.

Even in the mid-1960s other thoughts were occupying the minds of the Boeing designers. About this time the US government invited the company, together with Douglas and Lockheed, to submit proposals for a large transport aircraft

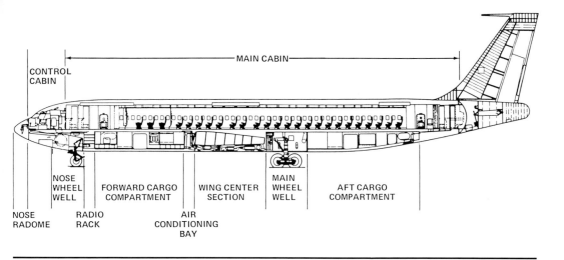

MAIN CABIN

CONTROL CABIN

NOSE WHEEL WELL

FORWARD CARGO COMPARTMENT

WING CENTER SECTION

MAIN WHEEL WELL

AFT CARGO COMPARTMENT

NOSE RADOME

RADIO RACK

AIR CONDITIONING BAY

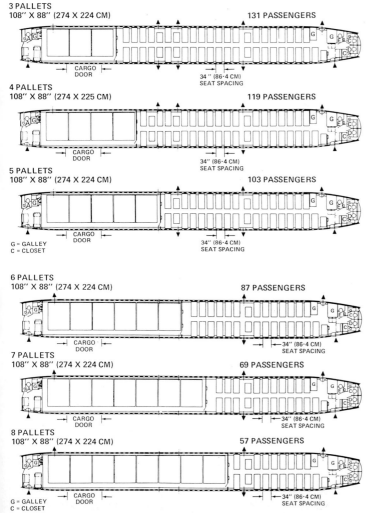

3 PALLETS
108" X 88" (274 X 224 CM)

131 PASSENGERS

CARGO DOOR

34" (86·4 CM) SEAT SPACING

4 PALLETS
108" X 88" (274 X 225 CM)

119 PASSENGERS

CARGO DOOR

34" (86·4 CM) SEAT SPACING

5 PALLETS
108" X 88" (274 X 224 CM)

103 PASSENGERS

CARGO DOOR

34" (86·4 CM) SEAT SPACING

G = GALLEY
C = CLOSET

6 PALLETS
108" X 88" (274 X 224 CM)

87 PASSENGERS

CARGO DOOR

34" (86·4 CM) SEAT SPACING

7 PALLETS
108" X 88" (274 X 224 CM)

69 PASSENGERS

CARGO DOOR

34" (86·4 CM) SEAT SPACING

8 PALLETS
108" X 88" (274 X 224 CM)

57 PASSENGERS

CARGO DOOR

34" (86·4 CM) SEAT SPACING

G = GALLEY
C = CLOSET

Above:
A 707-320C in a typical all-passenger configuration.

Left:
There were a number of layouts available for combi working.

37

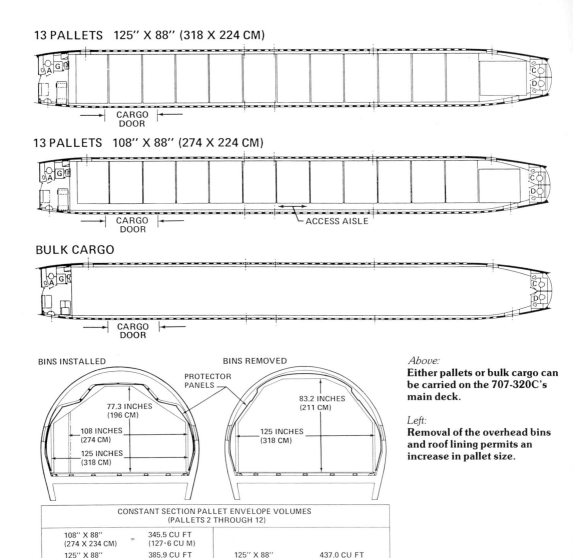

13 PALLETS 125" X 88" (318 X 224 CM)

CARGO DOOR

13 PALLETS 108" X 88" (274 X 224 CM)

CARGO DOOR — ACCESS AISLE

BULK CARGO

CARGO DOOR

BINS INSTALLED   BINS REMOVED

PROTECTOR PANELS

77.3 INCHES (196 CM)   83.2 INCHES (211 CM)

108 INCHES (274 CM)   125 INCHES (318 CM)

125 INCHES (318 CM)

Above:
Either pallets or bulk cargo can be carried on the 707-320C's main deck.

Left:
Removal of the overhead bins and roof lining permits an increase in pallet size.

CONSTANT SECTION PALLET ENVELOPE VOLUMES (PALLETS 2 THROUGH 12)			
108" X 88" (274 X 234 CM) =	345.5 CU FT (127·6 CU M)		
125" X 88" (318 X 234 CM) =	385.9 CU FT (10·93 CU M)	125" X 88" (318 X 234 CM) =	437.0 CU FT (12·38 CU M)

NOTE   ENVELOPES ALLOW FOR 0.75 INCHES (2 CM) CLEARANCE TO PALLET EDGE ON EACH SIDE AND 2.0 INCHES (5 CM) ON FORE AND AFT ENDS. PALLETS ARE 1 INCH (2·5 CM) THICK.

required for the USAF. Although unsuccessful in the competition, Boeing obtained a great deal of useful knowledge at the taxpayers' expense. It was a logical step to adapt the military project for a similar purpose in the commercial market, but by the spring of 1966 it had been further developed into a giant passenger airliner. As usual Pan American was willing to maintain its reputation as a pioneer by ordering the new wide-bodied 747 in April 1966, effectively sealing the fate of any future 707 variants.

So it was the Series 320C that had the distinction of becoming the last of the commercial family in production, which ended in 1979 after 813 of all models had been completed. A steady trickle of new airframes have since been built for military use as Airborne Warning & Control Systems (AWACS) which are based on the civil airliner design rather than the KC-135 tanker and derivatives. In the early 1980s there seemed a distinct possibility that the 707 would be one of the types to suffer from the proposed noise regulations. There was little interest by operators in the quieter and more efficient CFM56 range of engines, but as the deadline came nearer so alternative means were found to reduce the impact on ears by using redesigned nacelles and other devices. Still by no means as quiet as those equipped with later power plants, nevertheless the modifications brought the 707s within limits for continued service.

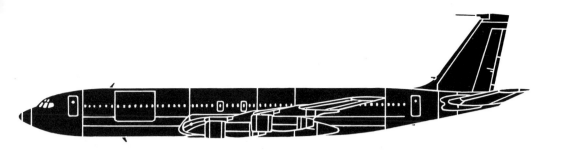

720 Development

At an early stage in the evolution of its commercial jet contender, Boeing realised that it would be necessary to include a short-to-medium range version to operate over sectors of up to 1,500 miles. As a member of the growing 707 family it was logical that it should be given a series number within the existing sequence. In appearance the 707-020 closely resembled the Model 120, which in its short-bodied form was 10ft (3.05m) shorter than the standard example most favoured by the airlines. But appearances can prove deceptive.

In fact by the time that the designers had completed their drawings the wing had been given a new profile with several detailed refinements, all aimed to improve the performance and handling of the aircraft. While retaining the same span as its larger relative, the section between the root and the inner pod was given a wider chord. Additional leading edge flaps were fitted to assist in shorter take-offs, a feature that was later introduced to the B variants of the 707. By using thinner gauge metals for some areas of the airframe together with a lighter undercarriage structure and reduced fuel capacity, a considerable weight saving was achieved. Even the Pratt & Whitney JT3C-7 engines played a part in this reduction, so with the

Below:
The prototype 720 on one of its early test flights. It eventually went into service with United Airlines.
Boeing Archives

same thrust developed the result was a distinctly more lively departure from the runway.

Although the fuselage had the same outline, at 136ft 2in (41.50m) in length, it was 1ft 8in (0.5m) longer than the smallest Series 120 and 8ft 4in (2.54m) shorter than the standard model. Its reduced capacity cabin was usually laid out with 38 first class seats plus another 74 in the economy section when employed for scheduled work. Because there were fewer passengers, Boeing found it possible to eliminate one of the three air conditioning units carried by the 707 to produce yet more weight savings. Also included on the production machines was the extended fin first developed for the Series 420 in order to provide better directional stability at low take-off and landing speeds. This model was also responsible for the rudder boost system fitted as standard to the whole family at an early stage. So many features were unique to the newcomer that the manufacturer decided that it warranted its own identity, so the 707-020 became the Model 720 with the sub-series number beginning at -020.

United Airlines became the first customer for the 720 which made its maiden flight on 23 November 1959. Certification trials for the FAA began on 18 January 1960, the prototype being joined by two others within a month or two. Together they accumulated 442hr of test flying of which 48 were specifically for the authorities. Although take-offs were demonstrated at an impressive 230,000lb, a lower maximum was decreed for the service specimens. After barely six months the 720 received its seal of approval which cleared the way for it to enter service with United on 5 July. The Los Angeles-Denver-Chicago route was the first to see the type, followed three days later by the Los Angeles-Seattle sector. Five aircraft had been with the carrier for some time before the type certificate was forthcoming, so there had been plenty of opportunity for training details prior to the introduction. United favoured a mixed-class configuration of about 105 seats, but American opted for a total of 98, of which 48 were in the first class section. This operator was able to start-up on 31 July choosing the Cleveland-St Louis-Los Angeles route as its first offering.

In the meantime, a more advanced model had been developed at Seattle which took to the air on 6 October. As in the case of the 707, the suffix B after the series number indicated that turbofans were fitted. Once again American had led the way by stipulating that 15 of its order for 25 aircraft would be 720Bs, with deliveries commencing during the first months of 1961. The year also saw the return of the carrier's original 10 machines to Boeing for updating, an exercise which followed the similar programme carried out on the airline's 707-120s. Now equipped with the 17,000lb thrust JT3D-1, the 720Bs needed even less runway before becoming airborne and their capacity was also increased to a maximum of 149 passengers. Later, when Pratt & Whitney managed to persuade the JT3D to produce another 1,000lb thrust, somehow enough spare space was found in the cabin to enable another 16 seats to be installed.

Despite its excellent performance and efficiency, Boeing only sold 154 examples of the aircraft. Of these, 89 were to the 720B standard although many of the earlier version were subsequently converted. Their early retirement from scheduled work was mainly due to the arrival of the even more cost-effective 727, but the type nevertheless became popular with the charter operators for IT work. Nowadays many of the survivors have been withdrawn from service to unselfishly donate usable parts for the welfare of the still-active KC-135s.

Left:
From Air Malta's launch in 1974 until March 1983 the carrier relied upon 720s for all its operations. This particular example (9H-AAL) joined the fleet in 1979 after a long career with Western Airlines. *AJW*

Below left:
A new lease of life was guaranteed this 720-023B when it was selected to serve as an engine test bed for Pratt & Whitney in 1985. For the first 10 years of its life it had been operated by American Airlines but in 1971 it moved to Beirut to become OD-AFQ with Middle East Airlines. Suprisingly it survived 14 years in this turbulent area before becoming C-FETB with the engine manufacturer.
G. W. Pennick

Below:
After some 10 years service with American Airlines, this 720-023B was sold to the Los Angeles Dodgers as a team transport. Reregistered N1R, it was eventually acquired by Boeing for spares purposes.
Sherlock/G. W. Pennick

Variants

367-80 Dash Eighty

Developed as a private venture initially, it became the prototype for the KC-135 tanker and the 707/720 series of airliners. One of its early tasks was to prove that it was suitable for flight refuelling, so a dispensing boom was quickly fitted to the underside of the rear fuselage. With the main test programme completed, the Dash Eighty was then employed by Boeing for a variety of experiments connected with future projects. As engine technology advanced, so the machine was flown with the latest power plant prior to its use in the production machines. In this

Below:
Later employed as an engine test bed, at one time the Dash Eighty carried a rear-mounted JT8D-1 during the development of the 727. *Boeing Archives*

way turbojets such as the Pratt & Whitney JT3C-1, JT3C-4 and JT4 were taken aloft at various times in its career. As the turbofan was evolved so the Dash Eighty found itself with the JT3D-1, acquiring the revised designation 367-80B as a result. Although it was very much involved in demonstrating the new features of the B and C series, its activities were not restricted to the 707 range. Many of the 727 design features were first tried on the uncomplaining prototype which was progressively fitted with the proposed leading edge flaps and slats and an aft-mounted JT8D-1 engine then under development for the new trijet. By September 1964 the number of wheels comprising the Dash Eighty's undercarriage had multiplied for soft field landing trials at Harper Dry Lake in California. A total of 20 supported the machine, four on the noseleg and

Left:
An engine icing-trials rig was carried at one point by the Dash-Eighty.

Below:
A conspicuous nose probe was necessary for the Dash Eighty's work with NASA.
Boeing Archives

Bottom:
Inevitably the Dash Eighty's proboscis proved too much of a temptation for the local artist!
Boeing Archives

Above:
Another nose variation for the good-humoured prototype together with other additional protuberances elsewhere.

eight on each of the two main bogies. A year later found the busy airframe moving into the modern age on behalf of NASA. Equipped with a 15ft nose probe, it was employed for low speed tests in connection with the development of the future supersonic transports. Valuable contributions con-

Below:
Soft field landings were successfully tested with the Dash Eighty equipped with additional wheels.
Boeing Archives

tinued to be made by the Dash Eighty until the end of the 1960s when it was honourably retired. During its 16 years it had flown on 1,691 occasions for a total of 2,350hr and had played a significant part in the expansion of modern air travel. Deservedly the aircraft was recognised as one of the 12 most significant aircraft of all time when it was presented to the Smithsonian Institute in May 1972.

Span: 129ft 8in (39.52m). *Length:* 127ft 10in (38.96m). *First engines:* Pratt & Whitney JT3P (11,000lb thrust).

707-020
See Model 720

707-120 (long body)

First of the production 707s to fly. Although not intended for long range work it was first used on transatlantic operations by Pan American on 26 October 1958. Many of the 60 built were later brought up to B standard with the installation of turbofan engines.

Span: 130ft 10in (39.87m). *Length:* 144ft 6in (44.04m). *Engines* (120/120B): Pratt & Whitney JT3C-6 (13,500lb thrust)/Pratt & Whitney JT3D-1 (17,000lb thrust).

707-120 (short body)

This version was similar to the standard -120 but possessed a fuselage 10ft shorter in length. It gave a better range and speed performance than the larger variant but of course it was at the cost of reduced capacity. Only seven were ordered, all going to Qantas which found the type eminently suitable for its thinner long-haul sectors. All were delivered during the summer of 1959 and two years later were brought up to B standard by the manufacturer.

Span: 130ft 10in (39.87m). *Length:* 134ft 6in (40.99m). *Engines* (120/120B): Pratt & Whitney JT3C-6 (13,500lb thrust)/Pratt & Whitney JT3D-1 (17,000lb thrust).

707-220

Intended for operations in hot and high localities, this version was a standard Series 120 but equipped with the more powerful JT4A engines. It was also available with a choice of fuselage lengths. Braniff became a customer for the variant when it ordered five for its South American routes, but these remained the sole examples built by Boeing. The first -220 flew on 11 June 1959 but crashed on 19 October before delivery to the airline. Subsequently the survivors served without further incident until they were sold in 1971.

Above:
Following a brief initial spell with Pan American, this Series 321 then passed through the hands of numerous operators before adopting the registration N2276X. *AJW*

Span: 130ft 10in (39.87m). *Length:* 144ft 6in (44.04m). *Engines:* Pratt & Whitney JT4A-3 (15,800lb thrust).

707-320

First of the breed to be truly intercontinental, this version first flew on 11 January 1959. It enabled Pan American to replace its -120s on the Atlantic routes and before long the type was also in service with rival carriers. Boeing produced 69 of the series before moving on to the turbofan B models.

Span: 142ft 5in (43.40m). *Length:* 152ft 11in (45.60m). *Engines:* Pratt & Whitney JT4A-3 and -5 (15,800lb thrust) and later JT4A-9 and -10 (16,800lb) or JT4A-11 and -12 (17,500lb).

707-320B

Even greater success came with the B version of the -320 which had the benefit of turbofan engines and additional leading edge flaps which dispensed with the need for the ventral fin of the modified -320s/-420s. Redesigned wingtips increased the span slightly but these produced less drag than their predecessors. With its large carrying capacity over long distances, the -320B became the popular choice of many airlines ensuring a healthy production run of 182. As later improvements were developed, so they were incorporated in the -320B which when modified became known as -320BA to denote Advanced.

Span: 145ft 9in (44.42m). *Length:* 152ft 11in (45.60m). *Engines:* Pratt & Whitney JT3D-3 (18,000lb thrust) or later JT3D-7 (19,000lb).

Lufthansa was the source of Air Zimbabwe's fleet of 707-330Bs in the early 1980s, the example illustrated being VP-WKR ex-D-ABOX. *AJW*

707-320C

Last of the range and also the best selling model, the C series was introduced by Boeing as a convertible. It first flew on 19 February 1963, entering service with Pan American in June. Some of the 335 aircraft built were completed as pure freighters with the cabin windows suitably blanked off. In all cases the forward fuselage sported a door measuring 11ft 2in × 7ft 7in (3.40m × 2.30m)

which greatly aided the loading of pallets and containers.

Span: 145ft 9in (44.42m). *Length:* 152ft 11in (45.60m). *Engines:* Pratt & Whitney JT3D-3 (18,000lb thrust) or later JT3D-7 (19,000lb).

707-420

When first marketed this variant was offered with Rolls-Royce Conway engines but was otherwise similar to the -320 airframe. It attracted orders from several carriers, BOAC being the largest customer. During the course of its trials for its British certificate, a number of quite extensive modifications had to be implemented including a taller fin, ventral bumper and power assisted rudder. These were later included as standard on the production line or as a retrospective action. Air India, El Al, Lufthansa and Varig also chose the variant of which 37 were eventually completed.

Span: 142ft 5in (43.40m). *Length:* 152ft 11in (45.60m). *Engines:* Rolls-Royce Conway 505 (16,500lb thrust) and later Conway 508 (17,500lb).

707-420B

A proposed model using the -320B's modified wing plus Conways that produced 21,000lb thrust was announced in 1962. This was really intended as the answer to the Douglas decision to proceed with the stretched DC-8-60 series, but in fact nothing came of the Boeing design.

Above left:
A loaded pallet being secured in the forward section of a 707 freighter. *British Caledonian*

Left:
Pallets can be easily loaded through the forward cargo door on the Series 320C. HeavyLift took delivery of N2215Y in March 1989. *HeavyLift*

707-520B

This designation was used for several ideas, none of which came to fruition. One embodied a fuselage 12ft (3.66m) or so longer than the -320 to be powered either by JT3D-5A of 21,000lb thrust or Conway turbofans, but the transformation would still have left it considerably shorter than the Californian-built competitor. A more modest stretch was considered for another -520 project. This time the fuselage was only about 8ft (2.44m) longer than the standard intercontinental model but was intended to carry 197 passengers over a much longer range.

707-620

Conceived after the demise of the -420B, the Series 620 possessed a 180ft (54.86m)-long fuselage capable in standard form of carrying 230 passengers over a range of 4,000 miles. Primarily intended for domestic schedules, the aircraft was to be powered by JT3D turbofans. As time passed, so too did the -620, to be replaced on the drawing boards by the -620B. This time the fuselage stretch had been taken to about 30ft (9.14m) and the capacity had grown to some 240 seats for use on non-stop transatlantic services. This project also remained a paper exercise.

707-700

In 1978 Boeing contemplated offering a 707 version to be powered by CFM International CFM56-1B turbofans giving 22,000lb thrust. This move followed studies carried out for the USAF

concerning the re-engining of the KC-135s; and although generally similar to the -320B, the -700 was intended for long range work. One civil airframe was equipped with the new engines and was first flown on 27 November 1979. Trials were completed during the following July but the lack of airline interest in this variant or modernised -320B/Cs sealed the fate of the project. Although there was an increase in weight, this penalty was more than offset by lower fuel consumption, reduced noise levels and less smoke emission.

707-820

Much earlier, Boeing had used this series number for several alternative designs. At 195ft (59.44m), a much longer fuselage than hitherto was proposed so that a maximum of some 275 passengers could be carried over a range of 5,000 miles. To drag its 410,000lb weight off the ground it was necessary to call upon the services of the 21,000lb JT3D-5 turbofan, but even these were discarded in favour

of the higher rated JT3D-15 of 22,500lb in the next phase of the project. Fuselage lengths of 198ft (60.35m) and 208ft (63.40m) were also planned for use on the very long routes of up to 7,000 miles. Boeing's market researchers estimated that if the model was launched the company would probably manage to sell up to 100. There was a reasonable amount of interest shown at quite an early stage, bringing an option for three from World Airways while Pan American had the right to change its existing -320B order to include the new variant if required. As time passed it became apparent that stretching the fuselage was not quite as straightforward as first thought. Airline support was also waning so in August 1965 the whole idea was abandoned.

720-020

Originally referred to as the 707-020, the aircraft was sufficiently different to warrant its own identity. Intended for intermediate range work the 720 had the ability to operate from relatively short runways with a high payload. This was achieved by introducing a refined wing design which included various flaps on the leading and trailing edges. Many saw service on the US domestic routes when first delivered, but later the variant was popular with charter companies in other parts of the world. The improved 720B provided still greater efficiency with its turbofan power but demand was limited so production ended in 1969 after a total of 154 of both models had been built.

Below:
The Luftwaffe ordered four new Series 307Cs for delivery in 1968, 10+03 being one of the batch.
Zastow via G. W. Pennick

Span: 130ft 10in (39.88m). *Length:* 136ft 9in (41.68m). *Engines:* Pratt & Whitney JT3C-7 (12,500lb thrust) or JT3D-1 (17,000lb) in the 720B.

Military derivatives
C-137/VC-137

Several Series 153 and -353 were acquired by the USAF for use as VIP transports.

C-18A/EC-18B

Modified ex-American Airlines Series 320Cs (N7563A/5A/6A/7A/9A/98A/N8401/03) for service as Advanced Range Instrumentation Aircraft.

E-3 Sentry

New airframes to -320C standard for use as AWACS aircraft by USAF, NATO, Saudi Arabia, France and the RAF. Saudi Arabia was also supplied with the KE-3 tanker variant.

E-6A Hermes

Sixteen ordered by the US Navy to use for communication links with its missile-carrying submarines.

E-8A

Secondhand Series 320C airframes modified for use on surveillance work.

49

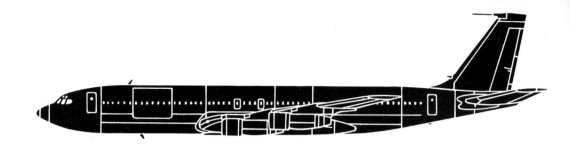

Unwelcome Incidents

Despite the lengthy design stages and the rigorous test programme which followed, with a new technology aircraft such as the 707 it was perhaps inevitable that problems would occur during the early stages of service. Also not unnaturally, any minor incident found its way into the pages of the press — usually grossly exaggerated or inaccurately reported.

The first such occasion came early in 1959 only a few weeks after the type's commercial baptism. Routine inspection of the airframe revealed a hairline crack on a splice-plate near the wing root. This offending item was due for replacement anyway and was only present on the first few machines off the line. Steel was originally specified for the component, but this was found less satisfactory than light alloy so its use was discontinued. Needless to say the mention of cracks brought references to the Comet disasters, which of course was completely misleading.

On the night of 3 February 1959 a more serious event took place which could have created a major unexplained mystery and considerable damage to the reputation of the 707. In charge of a Paris-New York flight, N712PA was some 500 miles east of Gander when the auto-pilot became disconnected. A Mach trim system was installed by Boeing specifically to provide positive longitudinal stability at speeds greater than the cruising speed on this flight, but for some unexplained reason this device had been switched off. There was therefore no warning or corrective action as the aircraft was directed towards the ocean in a spiral dive leaving the human crew to struggle with the controls, finally winning the battle when the 707 was within 6,000ft of the water. During its rapid 29,000ft descent severe buffeting was experienced due to the maximum speed limit being exceeded. This was

undoubtedly a most unpleasant sensation for all on board but at least the airframe could not be blamed. After the passengers were transferred to another aircraft, N712PA was ferried to Renton for a thorough check by the manufacturer. There it was found to have sustained some skin wrinkling, aileron and wing fillet damage plus some fuel cell leaks.

On 25 February a Pan American 707 featured in another incident, this time over France. After taking off on a training flight from Le Bourget, N709PA was set to demonstrate the aircraft's characteristics when nearing its minimum control speed. To facilitate this and at the same time simulate conditions experienced after an engine failure on take-off, both starboard power units were reduced to an idling state. While ambling along at 8,000ft, the speed was allowed to fall below the safe limit, whereupon the starboard wing dropped sharply to produce a stalled spiral dive. Although recovery was quickly achieved, it was not before an engine, complete with its nacelle and most of the pylon, had parted company with the 707. There was no other apparent damage so the hastily modified trijet was able to continue the sortie without difficulty, although the landing was made at Heathrow instead of Paris due to the availability of better repair facilities at London. Meanwhile across the Channel no doubt some bemused French farmer was marvelling at the wonders of modern fertilisers as he viewed the outsized pod!

Upon inspection it was found that the failure had occurred in a similar position to that on a specimen undergoing extreme side load tests at Seattle. Apart from a bent wing rib, no other structural damage was discovered so the company decided to execute the repair at Heathrow before returning the aircraft to service. Sadly N709PA's career with Pan

American was not destined to last beyond 8 December 1963. On this date, while negotiating a thunderstorm prior to landing at Philadelphia, an empty wing fuel tank was struck by lightning with disastrous results. Use of the more flammable JP4 fuel was considered largely responsible for the explosion and ensuing fire which cost the lives of 81 people.

Back in 1959 Pan American's N707PA left some of its wheels on the ground as it took-off on 12 July, forcing a landing to be made on a bed of foam at Idlewild airport, New York. Barely a month later it was the turn of American Airlines to suffer a loss when N7514A crashed near Calverton, NY. This was also indulging in a spot of simulated double engine failure on take-off when it developed a yaw from which it did not recover. It was a condition produced by swept wings at low speeds making control increasingly difficult. Similar circumstances caused the loss of Braniff's Series 227 N7071 even before it was delivered. An over-enthusiastic recovery from such a situation on 19 October caused the 707 to unload three of its power units. Although the Boeing training captain immediately took over and successfully managed to level the wings, it was necessary to reduce power on the remaining engine in order to maintain this attitude. Because of this virtual powerless state there was little more that could be done than to crash land, sadly killing four of the eight personnel on board.

Many of these early minor and major events were due to inexperience of crews flying the modern jets. Pilots were converting from piston-engined types which were often more forgiving than the new equipment, but as the service hours built up, so the number of incidents declined. Nevertheless accidents did continue at a rate that did little to inspire confidence in the new mode of travel. Better to arrive slowly than not at all was the philosophy of many, although the crashes prior to 1961 had not involved aircraft actually in service. This changed on 15 February when Sabena lost its Series 329 OO-SJB while it was on approach to Brussels. In this disaster there were 72 fatalities.

Just over a year later, on 1 March 1962, the American Airline's Series 123B N7506A was destroyed while performing a climbing turn just after take-off from Idlewild. Although the strictly observed noise regulations were suspected, investigations proved it was a fault in the rudder system that caused the loss of the aircraft and 90 passengers and crew when the machine fell into Jamaica Bay.

Even in 1962 bombs were not unknown causes for airliner crashes. Continental's Series 124 N70775 was the unfortunate victim of such a device on 22 May while flying at 37,000ft near Mt Carterville in the State of Iowa. This wanton act was responsible for 45 lives being lost.

Air France had the misfortune to lose two of its 707 fleet members in June. Orly was the scene of the first disaster which occurred during the take-off run of the Series 328, F-BHSM. Although travelling at considerable speed along the runway, the aircraft failed to become airborne so the attempt was abandoned. Unfortunately it was too late and 130 people were killed in the resultant crash. It was subsequently discovered that the variable incidence tailplane had been set in the wrong position, but whether this was due to human or mechanical error was never established. Only three months' service lay ahead for F-BHST when it was delivered in March because on 22 June it struck a mountain at Guadeloupe during a night descent. This latest tragedy was responsible for 112 lives.

Before the year had ended yet another 707 was written off. This example was a Series 441 operated by Varig as PP-VJB and this too hit a mountain during a descent which terminated some 19km south of Lima, Peru, and here another 97 people died. It had not been a good year for air safety generally and the 707 in particular.

Through the 1960s and 1970s the 707 continued to be involved in a fair share of incidents with a significant proportion taking place on take-off or landing. Premature touchdowns were quite common and when Pan Am's N454PA landed short of the 9,000ft runway at Pago Pago, Samoa, on 30 January 1974, it was the 15th jet of all types to become a total loss as a result of similar mishaps in the previous 12 months. Inevitably due to the capacity of the larger airliners, loss of life was frequently high. However the total number of 707s in service should not be forgotten when the figures are considered, although quantity is no reason for increases in accidents.

Even with the dwindling numbers of 707 still active in the late 1980s, the type is still involved in major incidents from time to time. There was a particularly bad patch beginning on 17 October 1988 when a Uganda Airlines Series 338C crashed while carrying out a night landing in poor visibility at Rome (Fiumicino). Having made two unsuccessful approaches to runway 34R, for the third attempt the pilot chose 34L, a strip without full landing aids. During the final stages 5X-UBC struck some buildings 1km from the airport's boundary, in so doing losing a wing and causing the fuselage to break into two sections. Fortunately the 707 was only carrying 45 passengers and seven crew, but of these 32 lost their lives.

Another landing accident involved the Nigerian operator General & Aviation Services. In this case 5N-AYJ was unable to land at Cairo due to bad visibility but during the course of diverting to Luxor, the fuel state necessitated an emergency landing. All eight of those on board were killed, a fate also suffered by five people on the ground.

Disasters come in threes it is said and in this case the third occurred during the afternoon of 8 February 1989. Independent Air's 707 N7231T was en route from Bergamo, Italy, to the Dominican Republic when it crashed into the 1,800ft mountain on the Azores island of Santa Maria. A refuelling stop had been planned at the nearby airport and it was during the course of its descent in cloud that the aircraft was lost together with 144 passengers and crew. None of these incidents were brought about by any malfunction of the airframe.

In addition to the in-service disasters, a number of other machines have been destroyed through no fault of their own. Generally they happened to be innocent victims caught by terrorist activities or actions by other extremist groups. The motley collection of fanatics lurking in the environs of Beirut airport has made this site particularly eventful for any based or even passing 707/720. Both Middle East Airlines and Trans Mediterranean have suffered losses through the years while other aircraft have received serious damage from time to time.

Below:
The story is on the side of the nose! Not strictly speaking a 707, but a KC-135A which has been used for non-military duties, 59-1481 was formerly in the service of the US Federal Aviation Administration and is now used by NASA for training astronauts in zero gravity conditions. *Weightless Wonder IV,* as the aircraft is named, is **based at Ellington AFB, Houston, Tx where this picture was taken during a maintenance check.** *Peter Gilchrist*

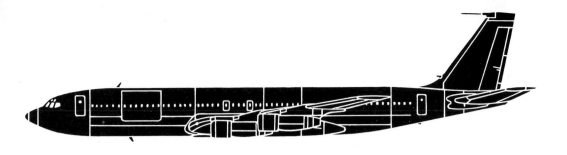

707s in Military Service

Although the 707 was primarily aimed at the civil market, at an early stage in its career the type was selected by the US authorities to replace the piston-engined veterans hitherto employed as Presidential transports. Three Series 153s were delivered to the 1298th Air Transport Squadron/1254th Air Transport Wing in May and June 1959, each configured with VIP interiors equipped with 22 seats. For this role the aircraft were allocated the designation VC-137A, although in 1963 all were modified to B standard when re-engined with Pratt & Whitney JT3D turbofans. By this time a fourth machine had been ordered and delivered, the newcomer being the larger Series 353B which was identified by the USAF as a VC-137C. Given the serial 62-6000, when it entered service in October 1962 this specimen became the well known Air Force One, a title derived from the radio call sign used when carrying the President. Conveniently based at Andrews AFB near Washington, it was responsible for the safe journeys of the US Heads of State both alive and dead until November 1972 when it was replaced by 72-7000, a later but similar 707-353B. All five C-137s — the V prefix was dropped during the time that President Carter was in power — remained in the charge of the 89th Military Aircraft Wing until the Presidential duties were taken over by a pair of 747s (VC-25A) from 1989.

Below:
When this VC-137A was delivered to the USAF in 1959 as 58-6971 it became a member of the 1254th Air Transport Wing/Military Air Transport Service. It is depicted in early MATS livery at San Francisco in April 1960. *Smalley/G. W. Pennick*

Delivered as a VC-137A in May 1959, 58-6971 was later brought up to B standard. *Boeing*

Left:
58-6971 climbing away at the start of another VIP mission.

Above:
Fourth of the VC-137 series, 62-6000 was delivered in October 1962 to be regularly used as the Presidential aircraft. One year later it was used to return the body of John F. Kennedy from Dallas after his assassination. *Boeing*

Operationally, transporting the nobility was little different from the normal commercial duties carried out by 707s, but acting as a flying radar station was not a pursuit originally envisaged for the type. Nothing is impossible it seems, because when Boeing and Douglas were invited to investigate the feasibility of installing advanced electronic equipment in either 707s or DC-8s in the late 1960s, it was the former that was chosen. A contract was awarded to the Seattle-based company for the conversion of two Series 320B airliners which upon completion were designated EC-137s by the USAF. There was no mistaking the pair because both carried a 30ft-diameter rotating antenna on two legs above the rear fuselage. Since two suppliers competed for the radar order, one of the aircraft

was fitted with the Westinghouse product, while Hughes supplied the equipment for the other machine. Both were ready for flight in early 1972, resulting in 71-1407 taking to the air on 9 February for a maiden sortie lasting 1hr 33min. Doubts about the possible aerodynamic effect of the rotodome proved unfounded, so during the next day the second EC-137D was also taken aloft.

Having confirmed that the 707 was willing to endure this unnatural addition to its structure, the

Below:
Interior view of the well-appointed Presidential aircraft, Air Force One in 1961. *US Air Force*

task of evaluating the rival radar systems began in earnest. From the start of the programme on 4 April until the final excursion on 5 September, 49 trips were made by each of the prototypes. They had flown in all weather conditions, by night and day, over sea and land and in hot and cold climates. It took the authorities a month or so to analyse the results, but in October it was announced that the Westinghouse system had been chosen for the proposed E-3A Airborne Warning & Control Systems (AWACS) aircraft.

There was still much development work required for which task both EC-137s were similarly equipped. Production of the initial batch of true E-3As was authorised in April 1975, with the first flight taking place at Seattle on 31 October. Unlike the other military 707s, the latest derivative was

almost windowless, so in this respect it resembled the KC-135. Deliveries began on 24 March 1977 to the 552nd Airborne Warning & Control Wing based at Tinker AFB, Ok, the unit becoming fully operational about one year later. All the machines were to E-3A standard and included amongst them were the two trials EC-137s now suitably refurbished.

By the end of 1980 funding had been authorised for 28 E-3As, but naturally the type was the subject of continuing improvement. A maritime surveillance facility was added after the 21st machine had been delivered, an enhancement subsequently introduced retrospectively to the earlier specimens. These updates of the avionics and other equipment were sufficient to warrant a change of designation to E-3B, but the last 10 of the eventual 34-aircraft order were given a C suffix by virtue of their additional crew display consoles, radio installations and improved anti-jamming devices. In due course the entire fleet will be brought up to this advanced standard, but obtaining the necessary allocation of funds is a slow and painful process.

The USAF AWACS operate worldwide in service with the 552nd Wing and are detached at Keflavik, Iceland and Kadena, Okinawa, although the majority remain at their home base in the US. During the course of a normal patrol the aircraft can remain aloft for between nine and 11hr, but by using the services of the supporting KC-135 tankers, the time can be doubled. Operating at 29,000ft, the E-3s maintain a cruising speed of Mach 0.72, a combination which gives the radar a range of over 230 miles against low-level targets.

Considering the enormous cost involved, it is surprising that any other sales were forthcoming. It was at an early stage that Iran emerged as a potential customer and was duly given the opportunity to acquire 10 AWACS at the end of 1975. This aroused the wrath of many opposed to such a deal, so to appease the critics the number was reduced to seven, none of which would contain anything remotely classified. No doubt there was considerable relief when the order was cancelled by Iran's new regime in 1979. Nevertheless a number of unmodified 707s were delivered to the Imperial Iranian Air Force in the 1970s.

More controversy accompanied Saudi Arabia's decision to acquire five E-3As in June 1983. This time the contract was duly signed although some argued that it would undermine Israel's security, an unlikely situation because the latter had already countered the risk by obtaining its own early-warning E-2C Hawkeyes. Saudi Arabia also ordered six KE-3A tankers to support the AWACS aircraft, a total subsequently increased by two. While flight-refuelling is their primary role, they also have the capability to operate on surveillance duties

if required. Handover of the first of the 13-strong CFM56-2-powered batch was completed on 30 June 1986 whereupon no time was lost in ferrying the machine via Mildenhall to its new home at Riyadh. Here it joined the recently-activated No 18 Squadron which, by the end of September 1987, had also received the remaining 12.

Second only to the USAF's fleet in terms of size, NATO operates 18 E-3As on its peace-keeping missions around the world. With so many nations involved there were interminable delays in the early stages of discussion before a decision was reached about the size of the order — if in fact there was a requirement at all. Years passed and prices increased but finally agreement was reached and the contract with Boeing was duly signed in 1978. As the aircraft were completed at Seattle, so they were flown to Oberpfaffenhofen, West Germany, for the installation of equipment by Dornier. In view of this multi-national ownership, all were registered in Luxembourg because this country had no air force of its own and therefore no national marks. As a result the E-3As have a mix of civil and military letters and numbers for identification purposes together with ample evidence of their NATO connections.

The postwar-built airfield at Geilenkirchen, West Germany, was earmarked as the future base for the

Below:
One of 34 E-3As operated by NATO, the all-white LX-N90449 was delivered in August 1983.
G. W. Pennick

AWACS force which was formally activated on 1 June 1982. However, it was mid-1985 before the unit became fully operational by which time all 18 aircraft had been delivered. Normally only a dozen or so E-3As are to be found at the headquarters site because it is necessary for the remainder to be out-stationed at more forward points to reduce travelling time to the operating areas. Preveza in Greece, Trapani in Italy and the Turkish airfield at Konya all regularly accommodate the AWACS, while the UK bases at Leuchars, Waddington and Wyton plus Keflavik in Iceland are used from time to time.

Unlike the Saudi machines, NATO's E-3As are powered by Pratt & Whitney 100A turbofans giving 20,500lb thrust. Although fuel costs could be reduced by re-engining the fleet with CFM56s, in view of the enormous expense involved it is thought the money would be better spent on updating the electronic gear within the aircraft. During 1986 some of the savings were invested in three ex-Sabena 707-329Cs (OO-SJL/N) for both crew training and transport duties. Upon delivery all were re-registered using a dual Luxembourg and US civil code to prefix the respective constructor's numbers to become LX-N19996, LX-N20198 and LX-N20199.

In the mid-1970s there was an intensive campaign mounted by Boeing to interest the UK government in the E-3A as a replacement for the ageing Shackletons. At the time it seemed that the American machine did not meet all the require- ments considered necessary so the British Aerospace/GEC Avionics Nimrod development was selected. Eleven aircraft were ordered in 1977 and it was expected that the first of the batch would be available for training in 1982. Problems encountered by GEC meant that the date steadily slipped back with no hope of any deliveries until the second half of 1987 at the earliest. Even if this was possible the aircraft would only be completed to trials standard. After checking the nation's financial

Above:
Three ex-Sabena 707s were acquired by NATO for crew training purposes. A combination of national codes prefix the constructor's number to produce LX-N20198. *G. W. Pennick*

state the Defence Minister announced that the programme had been terminated on 18 December 1986 and that six E-3As would be ordered.

Ten years had passed since the original approaches by Boeing and during this time some £660 million had been spent on the Nimrod and its avionics. Meanwhile the price of E-3As had naturally increased so that an expenditure of £860 million was necessary, a figure which included the initial support for the aircraft and its contents. This would rise to over £1,000 million if the RAF decided to take up its options on another pair. As a part of the deal, much of the work was to be sub-contracted to UK companies including British Aerospace which was also given the responsibility for flight testing before delivery to the RAF.

Below:
A USAF E-3A positions for refuelling from a KC-135.

Designated AEW Mk 1 Sentry, the first machine was rolled-out on 11 July 1989 and was due to achieve initial operating capability (IOC) in February 1990. In the following June, Waddington prepared to receive its first machine which was in fact the second production aircraft. Flight and equipment tests were then begun so that its IOC could be achieved, a procedure to be followed by the remainder of the batch. Assuming all goes well,

Above:
Although a retouched photograph of a CFM56-powered E-3A, it does give a reasonably realistic impression of a future RAF E-3A. Maybe the serial really will be hyphenated! *Boeing*

Below:
Popular with the Iranian Air Force, a number of 707s were purchased from Boeing in the 1970s for use as transports and tankers. *Boeing*

Above:
Regular visits were made to the UK by Argentine Air Force 707s prior to the Falklands disagreement.
AJW

it is intended that the Sentries will take over from the Shackletons from midnight on 30 June 1991. So some 15 years after the first negotiations, the RAF will have its modern AWACS aircraft. It is to be hoped that the wait and cost will be worthwhile.

Over the Channel the French had also contemplated the acquisition of its own early warning aircraft in the late 1970s. Although officially the merits of both the Nimrod and E-3A were considered, the customary reluctance to support anything British meant that the Boeing product was a clear-cut favourite. Any remote chance that the outsider would win was lost when the Nimrod project was cancelled. After extended negotiations three E-3As were ordered together with options for another two, one being taken up later in 1987. Since the French already had a fleet of C-135FRs which were powered by CFM56s, it was logical that this power plant should be specified for the newcomers. Perhaps the news that the RAF's E-3As were to be similarly endowed had not filtered through.

The US Navy is not normally associated with aircraft such as the 707, but on 3 August 1989 the first two of the order for 16 were formally handed over. Known as the E-6A, this derivative is intended to replace the EC-130Q Hercules currently used for communication links between missile-carrying submarines and their Washington control. First unit to receive the new equipment was VQ-3 located at Barber's Point, Hawaii, five aircraft being on strength by the end of October 1989.

During the flight trials programme some problems were encountered when the prototype shed a portion of its fin while carrying out flutter tests. Investigations revealed the cause of this unplanned event and the necessary remedial action taken. Subsequently at the end of September the aircraft proved this to be insufficient when once again it disposed of a sizeable section of its vertical tail. However, no restrictions were placed on the airframes already delivered and it was considered

unlikely to prevent the hand-over of all 16 on schedule.

Patuxent River-based VQ-4 was the second unit earmarked for the E-6A, although there is a distinct possibility that both units will eventually be merged and moved to Tinker AFB, Ok, where a support facility already exists for the USAF's E-3s. Since the windowless E-6As carry the same systems, it seems a sensible arrangement in the interest of economy and efficiency.

As deliveries of the E-6As were made, so the ousted Hercules were due to revert to their normal cargo-carrying role. This process was not quite as straightforward as could reasonably be expected because these particular machines were built without the normal rear loading ramp. Therefore a long and expensive programme of major surgery will be needed before they are fully operational in their more familiar guise, an undertaking which could have been overlooked by the authorities.

While Boeing has been steadily producing new airframes to meet these military orders, an increasing number of one-time civilian 707s have found themselves conscripted into air forces in various parts of the world. Many of these are used as VIP transports in a similar manner to the US C-137s, but others have undergone a more traumatic experience by becoming tankers for flight refuelling purposes. Although Boeing itself has marketed the version, the company has had to compete with Israeli Aircraft Industries which has handled a number of ex-airliners in the last 10 years or so. The familiar hose and drogue technique is employed by the 707s, with the necessary gear contained in either wingtip or underwing pods. With the ability to operate in the dual role of

transport and tanker, the rejuvenated 707s offer a relatively inexpensive solution for smaller nations.

Even the USAF has found the retired civilian airliners useful for its purposes. Between 1982 and 1984 eight -320Cs acquired from American Airlines joined the 4950th Wing at Wright Patterson AFB whereupon they were given the serials 81-0891 to 81-0898 inclusive and redesignated as C-18As. In due course the first of these was sent to E-Systems at Greenville, Tx, to be converted into an EC-18B for service as Advanced Range Instrumentation Aircraft (ARIA). After its inaugural flight in this guise on 27 February 1985, another three of the batch were ferried to Greenville for similar work to be carried out. All four ARIAs were due to be in service with the USAF by 1988 to replace the EC-135N fleet.

A similar decision was reached for future examples intended to carry the highly advanced Joint Surveillance Target Attack Radar System (J-STAR). Originally the airframes were to be new from the Boeing 707-320C production line in common with the E-3 and ex-civilian E-6As, but since the first flight of the variant in 1988, policy changes has meant that future specimens will be refurbished airliners. Grumman Melbourne Systems Division was given the responsibility for developing

Above:
This 707-347C was not taken up by Western Airlines so was diverted to the Canadian Air Force as 13702 in 1970. *AJW*

and installing the radar equipment; the lengthy test programme being scheduled for completion in 1991. In the meantime a second prototype (86-0471) first flew in August 1989 to take its place in the avionics test programme. When operational the E-8s' role will be to maintain surveillance of any hostile territory from a safe distance.

As a result of the revived interest in secondhand machines, the 707 has found an unexpected new lease of life. Under the circumstances Boeing has finally decided to terminate the type's long run which will now end with the roll-out of the last RAF Sentry in May 1991. It certainly means that the 707 in one form or another will be seen for many more years to come.

Below:
Earmarked to become an EC-18B, 81-0894 was a Series 323C with American Airlines until retired in 1981. After a period in store the 707 was sold to the USAF at which point it was designated a C-18A.
D. Menard/G. W. Pennick

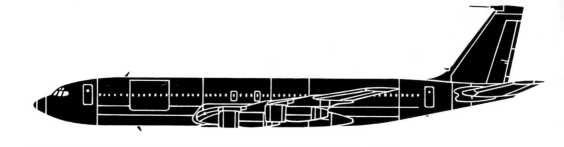

707/720 Customer Numbers

At an early stage Boeing devised a system of customer codes for identification purposes. This was achieved by allocating the second two digits of the three figure series indicator to individual airlines. In this way Pan American's 707 Series 120s and 320s became 121s and 321s respectively. Similarly 27 was reserved for Braniff, so its Series 220s were known as -227s and the later machines became -327s. These identities are retained throughout the aircraft's life and are also applied in the same manner to other types such as the 727, 737, etc. When Boeing had used all 100 number combinations, the company began a new batch in the range A0 to A9, B0 to B9, etc. They were dispensed in exactly the same manner as before.

07 West German Air Force
09 China Airlines
11 Wardair
12 Malaysian-Singapore/Singapore
    International Airlines
21 Pan American
22 United Airlines
23 American Airlines
24 Continental Airlines
25 Eastern Air Lines
27 Braniff
28 Air France
29 Sabena
30 Lufthansa
31 Trans World Airlines
36 British Overseas Airways Corporation/
    British Airways
37 Air India
38 Qantas
39 Cubana
40 Pakistan International
41 Varig
44 South African Airways

45 Seaboard World
47 Western Airlines
48 Aer Lingus
49 Flying Tiger Line
51 Northwest Orient
53 USAF
55 Executive Jet
58 El Al
59 Avianca
60 Ethiopean Airways
62 Pacific Northern
65 Cunard Eagle
66 United Arab Airlines/Egyptair
68 Saudia
69 Kuwait Airways
70 Iraqi Airways
72 Airlift International
73 World Airways
79 Saturn
82 TAP-Air Portugal
84 Olympic Airways
85 American Flyers
86 Iran Air
87 Aerolineas Argentinas
96 Quebecair
99 Caledonian Airways
B4 Middle East Airlines
B5 Korean Airways
D3 Alia/Royal Jordanian
F3 Portuguese Air Force
F9 Nigeria Airways
H7 Cameroon Airlines
J6 CAAC
J8 Sudan Airways
J9 Imperial Iranian Air Force
K1 Tarom
L5 Libyan Government
M1 Pelita
P1 Ruler of Qatar
W6 Government of Morocco

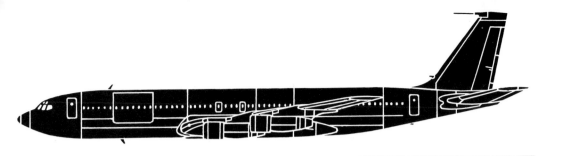

Operators

Many of the operators which have used the 707 or 720 through the years are listed in this section. The aircraft recorded were not necessarily in the fleets at the same time because some carriers constantly leased specimens for short periods as the need arose, but they have been included for the record where known. In the spring of 1989 there were still about 210 examples of the 707 distributed thinly amongst some 80 airline and government operators. These are indicated in the following by means of a * after the company's title. Brief details of the individual machines used contain type, series, constructor's number and registration.

Aerlinte Eireann/Aer Lingus
Results from its US services encouraged the airline to order three new 720s in 1959. Because of the shorter distance involved by operating from Shannon, the type was considered suitable for the transatlantic sectors. After the delivery of the first machine in October 1960, the inaugural commer-

cial service was flown on 14 December when EI-ALA left Dublin for New York. These schedules were maintained by the type until 1964 when the larger and longer range 707-348s took over. Much of the Irish flag carrier's traffic was seasonal so both the 720s and 707s were leased to other companies throughout their careers. Towards the end the survivors were used for IT work, until finally in October 1986, EI-ASO became the last to leave the airline's fleet.

707-348C: 18737 (EI-AMW), 18880 (EI-ANO), 19001 (EI-ANV), 19410 (EI-APG). **707-349C:** 18976 (EI-ASN), 19354 (EI-ASO). **720-048:** 18041/43 (EI-ALA/C)

Below:
Delivered to the Musee de l'Air at Le Bourget in 1983, the 707-328B is displayed in its Air France livery as F-BLCD. *A. S. Wright*

AeroAmerica

A large fleet of 707s and 720s was assembled by this US airline after it was formed in January 1974. These were flown from the company's base at Seattle and its out-stations at Cairo and West Berlin during the course of extensive IT and charter operations. Both domestic and international scheduled services were also introduced in the late 1970s and the company held the licences for several others such as the Berlin-Saarbrücken sector. This all came to an end in November 1979 when the authorities revoked the operator's certificate due to doubtful financial and safety aspects. A new start was made with one 720, but by 1984 AeroAmerica had ended its career for the second time.

707-123B: 17648/9 (N7521A/2A). **707-138B:** 17700 (N793NA). **707-131:** 17662 (N735T). **707-227:** 17694 (N64740). **707-321:** 17592 (N714FC), 17597 (N431MA). **707-321B:** 18833 (N402PA), 18835 (N404PA). **707-331:** 17686 (N705PA). **720-022:** 17907 (N7201U), 17913 (N7207U). **720-027:** 18064 (N736T), 18065 (N734T), 18154 (N730T), 18423 (N731T), 18581 (N733T). **720-038:** 18042 (N303AS). **720-048:** 18041 (N1776Q). **720-062:** 18377 (N302AS)

Aerocondor

At one time Aerocondor was Colombia's second largest international airline, using 707s for services to the US, Netherlands Antilles and Ecuador. In October 1980 the company ended its operations due to severe financial difficulties and all route licences were taken over by other carriers.

707-123B: 17637 (HK-1818), 17638 (HK-1802, 17643 (HK-1942). **720-023B:** 18023 (HK-1973), 18028 (HK-1974)

Aero Filipinas

One 707 comprised the fleet of this airline when it was formed in 1981 to provide passenger charter services from Manila to other points in the Far East and Gulf States. When the aircraft was sold in 1985 the airline also ceased its operations.

707-351C: 19034 (RP-C1886)

Aerolineas Argentinas*

Four 707s were ordered in 1965 for delivery during the following year. In the event the first schedule using the type was flown on 15 December 1966 followed by the introduction of a non-stop New York run on 2 February 1967. European services were also taken over by the 707s, two more joining the fleet in each of 1968 and 1971. Towards the end of the 1970s the arrival of the 747 saw the gradual release of the earlier type, most of which were transferred to the Argentine Air Force. One

has remained with the airline (LV-ISC) for cargo work although on occasions it has been leased out.

707-372C: 20076/77 (N738AL/9AL – became LV-LGO/P). **707-387B:** 19238/41 (LV-ISA/D), 19961/2 (LV-JGR/P)

Aeropa

Previously known as Societa Aerea Veneziana, Aeropa came into being in July 1973 for the purpose of operating IT and charter flights from Rome. Two 707s were used, but the enterprise was short-lived because in February 1975 the Italian authorities refused to renew the carrier's licence.

707-131: 17664 (I-SAVA). **707-321:** 17594 (N716HH)

Aerotal Colombia

It was 1979 before Aerotal leased its first 707 for use on its scheduled passenger and cargo services. As the network grew a 720 arrived together with several other 707s for the newly introduced Miami sector. Their careers with the carrier ended in 1984 when operations were ceased.

707-321: 17605 (N70798/HK-2410). **707-323C:** 19575 (HK-2842X). **707-373C:** 18709 (HK-2606X). **720-030B:** 18060 (HK-2558)

Aero Uruguay

Cargolux provided both aircraft and expertise for Aero Uruguay when it was formed in 1977. Later the same company leased a 707 to the cargo carrier but its temporary career was terminated in late 1981, just before the airline's operations met the same fate. Subsequently the title was resurrected in 1988 when a new charter company was formed.

707-321C: 18716 (CX-BPQ). **707-331C:** 19212 (CX-BJV)

Air Afrique

Created in 1961 by a consortium from a number of West African states with strong French ties, it was natural that there was a need to maintain the air links with Europe. Although the chosen type to operate the services was the DC-8, while awaiting delivery Air Afrique leased 707s from Air France to cover peak periods. Their stay was often only for a few weeks, but nevertheless they were duly allocated new registrations with a TU- prefix. This arrangement continued on an intermittent basis for some years.

707-328: 17922 (TU-TBY), 17924 (TU-TDC), 18245 (TU-TDB). **707-328B:** 18457 (TU-TXA/TU-TXB), 18458 (TU-TXF/TU-TXJ), 18686 (TU-TXI/TU-TXM), 19291 (TU-TXL/TU-TXN)

Above:
Showing signs of recent paint removing activity, this 707-331B was used by Air Berlin in 1981 as N8729. *G. W. Pennick*

Air Algerie

One 707 was leased from Pakistan International between February and May 1972 when there was a need for greater capacity. There has been no reoccurrence of the exercise.

707-340C: 19286 (AP-AUP)

Air Atlantis

See TAP-Transportes Aereos Portugueses

Air Berlin

This American airline began operations in April 1979 to provide passenger charters from Berlin/ Tegel to various holiday areas in Europe, Africa and the US. During the first year two 707s were bought from TWA, but at the end of 1980 they were sold to Aviation Traders at Stansted for spares use. Two other examples were leased during the same year, but these had left the company by the end of the 1981 summer season. Thereafter Air Berlin concentrated on European ITs using 737s.

707-123B: 17636 (N7509A). **707-331:** 17676 (N763AB), 17682 (N767AB). **707-331B:** 20058 (N8729)

Air Cargo Egypt

During its first two years or so Air Cargo Egypt used a leased DC-8 for its cargo charters, but in 1979 a 707 was acquired which then remained with the airline until operations ended in 1985.

707-338C: 18810 (SU-BBA)

Air Ceylon

See Air Lanka

Air Commerz Flug

This Hamburg-based carrier was formed in June 1970 to begin operations in October 1971. Worldwide passenger and cargo charters and IT services were flown by a pair of 707s originally owned by Qantas. However, their operational life with the company was short, because in September 1972 Air Commerz went into liquidation due to financial troubles and all operations were ceased.

707-138B: 17697 (D-ADAP), 17701 (D-ADAQ)

Air Congo

Formed in 1961, the airline operated several international routes although its busiest was the link with Brussels. A 707 was therefore leased from Sabena to maintain the schedules until such time that the carrier's own aircraft could cope with the declining traffic. When this point was reached the leasing arrangement still continued on an occasional basis even after Air Congo was renamed Air Zaire in October 1971.

707-329: 17626 (OO-SJD), 18374 (OO-SJF), 18460 (OO-SJG), 18890 (OO-SJH), 20198 (OO-SJM)

Air France

As the first customer for the 707-320 series, the airline was able to introduce the type on to its Atlantic services on 2 February 1960. This pioneer route was followed at regular intervals by others as more aircraft were received from Boeing. When the longer range Series 328Bs came on strength at the end of 1962, it permitted the introduction of non-stop sectors between Paris and Los Angeles, a schedule which previously made a transit stop at Montreal. Although the advent of the 747 meant that the 707s were gradually replaced on the main routes, the type continued with Air France into the 1980s. Many were scrapped during the previous decade while others found their way into the hands of new owners and still survive in various parts of the world.

707-328: 17613/22 (F-BHSA/J), 17918/24 (F-BHSK/Q), 18245/7 (F-BHSR/T), 18375 (F-BHSU). **707-328B:** 18456/9 (F-BHSV, F-BHSX/Z), 18685/6 (F-BLCA/B), 18941 (F-BLCD), 19291 (F-BLCE). **707-328C:** 18881 (F-BLCC), 19292 (F-BLCF), 19521/2 (F-BLCG/H), 19723/4 (F-BLCI/J), 19916/7 (F-BLCK/L). **707-355C:** 19986 (F-BJCM)

Air Frêt

This French company first progressed from piston engines to jets in 1976 when it obtained an ex-TWA 707 for its cargo charter work. These were operated from Nimes-Garons to various points in Europe and the Middle East, but all activities ceased in early 1982.

707-131: 17658 (F-BUZJ)

Air Florida

Air Florida began operations in September 1972 using a pair of 707s leased from Pan American. It was a strange choice of equipment because the carrier's modest route network only linked Miami with Tampa and Orlando, all within the State of Florida. It was not long before the unsuitability of the jet became apparent, so the pair were returned to their owner in March 1973 to be replaced by something more appropriate.

707-331: 17686 (N705PA), 17689 (N706PA)

Air Guinée

A 707 joined the airline's fleet in 1979 to take over some of the international services flown to Sierra Leone, Liberia, Mali and Senegal. Although a second arrived in 1981, it moved on after one year to leave the original machine to continue the duties until it too was retired in 1986.

707-328B: 19291 (3X-GCC). **707-351C:** 18748 (3X-GAZ)

Air Hong Kong*

Long-haul cargo services were begun by the carrier in 1988 using a 707 for the regular trips to Europe. It was joined by another of the breed (VR-HKL) during 1989.

707-321C: 19367 (VR-HKL). **707-336C:** 20517 (VR-HKK)

Air India

By May 1962 Air India had replaced its entire fleet with 707s which were then used to good effect to reduce flying times on its long haul routes to New York, London and Moscow. Unlike the majority of carriers, Air India ordered the Conway-powered Series 437 initially, although subsequent deliveries featured the more common JT3D engines. Unlike the first batch which suffered a number of incidents,

the Series 337B/Cs survived to serve the airline to the mid-1980s by which time they were due for honourable retirement if not scrapping.

707-337B: 18708 (VT-DPM), 18873 (VT-DSI), 19247 (VT-DVA). **707-337C:** 19248 (VT-DVB), 19988 (VT-DXT). **707-437:** 17722/24 (VT-DJI/K), 18055 (VT-DMN), 1841/5 (VT-DNY/Z)

Air Jamaica
Before its reorganisation into the present company in 1968, Air Jamaica operated 707s leased from BOAC. These retained their UK registrations and were taken at random from the fleet.

Air Lanka/Air Ceylon
In 1977 Air Ceylon leased a 720 for use on some of its international services which were growing in number. Operations were suspended in March 1978 due to heavy losses, but in the following January, Air Lanka took over the responsibilities of the national carrier with two 707s. These continued in service until the advent of TriStars in 1981.

707-312B: 19737/8 (4R-ALB/A). **720-023B:** 4R-ACS

Airlift International
Originally known as Riddle Airlines when formed in 1945, Airlift carried out extensive passenger, cargo and military charters with a number of leased 707s pending delivery of its ordered DC-8s. At this point the Boeings were released and there was no further involvement with the type.

707-355C: 19417 (N525EJ). **707-365C:** 19416 (N737AL). **707-372C:** 20076/7 (N738AL/9AL)

Air Madagascar
With Air France owning a considerable share of the airline, not surprisingly the French carrier supplied a

707 for the regular link with Paris. The type was used until 1979 when Air Madagascar took delivery of a new 747 whereupon the 707 returned to its original owner.

707-328: 17918 (F-BHSK). **707-328B:** 18686 (F-BLCB/5R-MFK)

Air Malta
Malta's national carrier commenced operations on 1 April 1974 using two 720Bs on lease/purchase from Pakistan International, the latter also supplying much of the expertise needed to run the airline in the early days. An extensive network of scheduled services was begun and it was not long before the carrier's fleet had grown to five 720s plus various other types on short leases when necessary. Although the arrival of the first 737s in the early 1980s relieved the situation, the 720s were retained for use on IT work until the final specimen (9H-AAO) was retired in November 1989.

707-123B: 17640 (9G-ACN), 17651 (9G-ACO). **707-3F5C:** 20515 (CS-TBU). **720-040B:** 18378 (AP-AMG/9H-AAM), 18380 (AP-AMJ/9H-AAN). **720-047B:** 18063 (9H-AAK), 18167 (9H-AAL), 18827 (TF-VLB), 18829 (9H-AAO)

Air Manila
A number of routes within the Philippines and to Indonesia were operated by the carrier in the late 1960s/early 1970s. Negotiations with TWA won a three years' advisory service for the inexperienced management and a pair of 707s, which in the event were never delivered. Financial troubles in 1973 brought a reorganisation which included the transfer of its existing domestic network to Philippine Air Lines. Other 707s were acquired to enable Air Manila to concentrate on longer haul charters to the US but by 1983 operations had ceased.

707-321: 17604 (RP-C7074), 17606 (RP-C911). **707-321B:** 18335/6 (RP-C7076/5). **707-331:** 17680 (RP-C7073)

Air Mauritius
International services to London and other European cities were operated with a British Airways/British Airtours 707 for some years. This arrangement ended when Air Mauritius acquired its own machine in 1981; a second 707 joining it two years later.

707-465: 18372 (G-ARWD). **707-344B:** 18891 (3B-NAE), 19133 (3B-NAF)

Below:
For several years BA's 707-465 operated in Air Mauritius' livery but retained its UK identity, G-ARWD. *AJW*

Air Niugini

Operations began in October 1973 mainly on domestic routes but Port Moresby was also linked with a number of Australian centres. At first a 720 was employed but later 707s took over the duties.

707-338C: 19294 (P2-ANH), 19621/2 (P2-ANB/A). **720-023B:** 18014 (P2-ANG)

Air Portugal

See TAP-Transportes Aereos Portugueses

Air Rhodesia

See Air Zimbabwe

Air Rwanda*

The national carrier contents itself with domestic services and visits to neighbouring countries. A 707 is employed as a freighter for long-haul charters which normally take it to Brussels or Mombasa.

707-328C: 19292 (9XR-JA)

Air Seychelles*

Founded in 1977, the Government-owned national carrier concentrated on inter-island services at first, but in October 1983 intercontinental schedules were introduced between Mahe and London via Frankfurt. For several years leased aircraft were employed, but in 1987 the company purchased two hush-kitted 707-324s known as Super Qs. These now fly non-stop between the Seychelles and

Europe to serve London, Frankfurt, Zurich, Rome and Athens and although a 767 was delivered in 1989, it is expected that the 707s will remain in use for some time in the future.

707-324C: 19869 (S7-2HM), 19871 (S7-4HM)

Air Siam

Various international services were operated by Air Siam in the late 1960s/early 1970s but were suspended in January 1972. Later in the year a restart brought a 707 into use for the Bangkok-Hong Kong-Tokyo schedules. In 1975 the type was replaced by a 747 and DC-10 but in any case the airline ceased operations in December 1976.

707-131: 17663 (HS-VGC), 17666 (HS-VGA)

Air Transcontinental/Transasian Airlines

This company was known as Transasian Airlines when formed in 1977, its main occupation being to provide aircraft for lease to other companies. On 22 August 1979 its name was changed and at the same time news was released that it proposed to enter the IT market from March 1980 by flying from

Below:
Acquired by Air Seychelles in 1987, the one-time Continental 707-324C N47331 was modernised and equipped with hush-kitted engines prior to delivery as N112HM. Before entering service it was re-registered S7-2HM. *G. W. Pennick*

Belfast, Manchester and Gatwick with its four-strong 707 fleet. Plans were changed abruptly in January following an acute money shortage which swiftly took the carrier into liquidation.

707-123B: 17640 (G-TJAB), 17651 (G-TJAC). **707-139B:** 17903 (G-TJAA). **707-321B:** 18337 (N762TB)

Air Viking

Keflavik, Iceland, was the base of this 720-equipped carrier when it was formed in March 1974. Fourteen months later its IT and charter operations were ceased but the aircraft were taken over by a similar company, Eagle Air, when it was launched in April 1976.

720-022: 18075 (TF-VVB), 18082 (TF-VVA). **720-025:** 18163 (TF-VVE)

Air Zimbabwe/Air Rhodesia*

Domestic and regional scheduled services became the main interest for Air Rhodesia after it was formed in 1967. With traffic expanding, three 720s were acquired in 1973 which remained with the carrier after the airline's name change in 1979. Long-haul services were introduced in 1980 coinciding with the arrival of 707s. These were employed throughout the 1980s although the delivery of a 767 in 1989 marked a reduction in use.

707-344B: 18891 (VP-WKW). **707-330B:** 18819 (VP-WKR/Z-WKR), 18923 (VP-WKS/Z-WKS), 18927 (VP-WKV/Z-WKV), 18929 (VP-WKT/Z-WKT), 18930 (VP-WKU/Z-WKU). **720-025:** 18162 (VP-YNL/Z-YNL), 18242 (VP-YNM/Z-YNM), 18244 (VP-YNN/Z-YNN)

Below:
When the Zimbabwe national code was changed, the flag carrier adopted a more striking livery as shown by Z-WKU ex D-ABUH. *AJW*

Alaska Airlines

A number of small carriers amalgamated to form Alaska Airlines, a title adopted in 1944. A new venture was attempted in 1970 when a series of charters to Siberia were introduced. A 707 was leased for the purpose and the exercise was repeated during the next couple of years. By 1973 the airline was beginning to build up a scheduled network with a fleet of Boeing 727s so the Russian trips were terminated with no further involvement with the 707.

707-138B: 17700 (N793SA). **707-321:** 17602 (N724PA), 17605 (N727PA). **720-024B:** 18416 (N57201)

Alia-Royal Jordanian*

Established in 1963, Alia began scheduled services to points throughout the Middle East and to the major centres in Europe. Two 707s were ordered in 1969, for delivery in early 1971. Although the airline later acquired more of the type, all were secondhand from such as Olympic and Pan American. Three examples are still operated by the Jordanian carrier.

707-321C: 18716 (JY-AED), 18767 (JY-AEE), 20017 (JY-AES). **707-344C:** 19706 (JY-AFR), 20283 (JY-AFQ). **707-384C:** 18948 (JY-AEB/JY-AJK), 18949 (JY-AEC). **707-3D3C:** 20494 (JY-ADO/P). **720-030B:** 18250/1 (JY-ADS/T)

Alyemda-Democratic Yemen Airlines*

The national airline operates from Aden to centres in the Gulf States, the Middle East, Africa and India using a pair of 707s for the latter schedules.

707-338C: 20374 (70-ACO). **707-369C:** 20547 (70-ACS)

American Airlines

On 25 January 1959 American began scheduled services with its new 707s on its longer sectors such as New York-Los Angeles. The carrier had ordered

American Eagle had a very brief existence in 1980/1981, so it followed that N404PA's stay was equally short. *AJW*

30 aircraft in November 1955 to become one of the launch customers so had the advantage for a time over its domestic competitors. Always willing to sponsor new developments, American was largely responsible for the more powerful B series of both the 707 and 720. Both variants were introduced by the airline on 12 March 1961 and eventually all of American's machines were brought up to the more advanced standard by Boeing. At its peak the carrier's fleet of 707/720s was one of the largest in the world, many remaining in service well into the 1980s.

707-123: 17628/52 (N7501A/25A), **707-123B**: 18054 (N7526A), 18882/5 (N7550A/53A), 19185 (N7554A), 19186/8 (N7570A/72A), 19323/44 (N7573A/94A). **707-323B**: 20170/9 (N8431/40). **707-323C** 18689/92 (N7555A/8A), 18938/40 (N7559A/61A), 19235/7 (N7562A/4A), 19380/4 (N7565A/9A), 19515/9 (N7595A/9A), 19574/7 (N8411/4), 19581/6 (N8401/6), 19587/9 (N8408/10), 20087/9 (N8415/7). **707-385C**: 19433 (N8400). **720-023**: 18013/22 (N7527A/36A). **720-023B**: 18023/37 (N7537A/51A). The 707-123s and 720-023s were later converted to -123Bs and -023Bs

American Eagle Airlines
Authorisation was given to the newly formed airline to commence worldwide charters in March 1980. Scheduled rights were obtained for services between the US and Germany but for a start a domestic schedule was introduced in the spring of 1981 to link Cleveland with Detroit. Hardly had it begun than it was suspended together with all other operations. With all speed the 707s were repossessed thereby ensuring the complete demise of the airline.

707-321B: 18833 (N402PA), 18835 (N404PA), 18839 (N408PA)

American Flyers
Formed in 1939 as a US supplemental airline, American Flyers ordered one 707 in 1966. A change of policy brought DC-8s into the fleet so the Boeing machine was sold to American Airlines before delivery.

707-385C: 19433 (N8400)

American Overseas Airways
See Guy American Airways

American Trans Air
Domestic and worldwide charter services were begun in 1981 using a fleet of 707s. After a busy four years or so all were retired at the end of 1984 to giveway to DC-10s and TriStars.

707-123B: 17642 (N7515A), 19185 (N7554A), 19186 (N7570A), 19323 (N7573A), 19339 (N758-9A). **707-323C**: 19517 (N7597A), 19519 (N759-9A), 20088 (N8416)

Anglo Cargo Airlines*
Based at Gatwick, Anglo began its worldwide cargo charter operations with one 707 in January 1984. Since then it has also been operating scheduled flights under contract to British Airways. A second aircraft was acquired in 1989.

707-338C: 19294 (G-EOCO), 19296 (G-BDEA)

Angola Air Charter*
See TAAG Angola

Arab Air Cargo

In 1981 the governments of Iraq and Jordan jointly formed Arab Air Cargo to operate both scheduled and cargo services in conjunction with Alia. A 707 was transferred from the two parent carriers so that from 1 May 1983 Amsterdam, Brussels, Dubai, Larnaca, London and Rome were served on a regular basis. The arrangement ended in 1989.

707-321C: 18716 (4YB-CAB). **707-370C:** 20890 (4YB-CAC)

Arkia*

In one form or another, Arkia has been in existence since 1950. In addition to scheduled domestic services, the airline also provides IT charter flights from Israel to a variety of European destinations using 707s leased from El Al.

707-331B: 18985 (4X-ATD). **707-336C:** 20456 (4X-BMC). **707-358B:** 19004 (4X-ATR), 19502 (4X-ATS). **707-358C:** 20122 (4X-ATX), 20301 (4X-ATY). **707-458:** 18071 (4X-ATB)

Arrow Air

When the airline was reactivated in 1980 it was equipped with a varied collection of 707s. Cargo charters were the first to start, but in 1981 the carrier began to operate passenger flights which included schedules between Denver and London on behalf of Western Airlines. By 1985 there had been a complete fleet change and Arrow had become a DC-8/10 operator.

707-321B: 20020 (N881PA). **707-321C:** 19271 (N707HT). **707-324C:** 19352 (N707JJ), 19353 (N707SH). **707-327C:** 19529 (N707AD), 19530 (N707ME). **707-338C:** 18808 (N707GB), 18809 (N4225J), 19294 (N707HW). **707-347C:** 19964 (N707PD)

Atlanta Skylarks

See Independent Air Transport

Above:
Arab Air Cargo's 707-370C 4YB-CAC was flown on the carrier's freight charter services between the Middle East and Europe. *AJW*

Austrian Airlines

Transatlantic services were started by Austrian Airlines in 1969 using a 707 leased from Sabena. However, the venture did not prove economic so the regular visits to New York were ended and the aircraft returned to its owner.

707-329: 18374 (OE-LBA)

Avianca*

Prior to the arrival of its own aircraft, Avianca leased a Pan American 707 to start-up its New York-Bogata services in 1960. When 720s were delivered in 1961 the airline expanded its network in the Americas and also to Europe. As traffic increased so the smaller type was replaced by the 707, several examples of the latter still serving with the carrier.

707-121: 17590 (N711PA). **707-321B:** 19266 (HK-2070X), 19276 (HK-2016), 19361 (HK-2015). **707-321C:** 18714 (HK-1718X), 18766 (HK-1849), 19375 (HK-2473). **707-359B:** 19741 (HK-1402), 20340 (HK-1410). **720-030B:** 18059 (HK-676), 18248 (HK-749). **720-047B:** 18061 (HK-723). **720-059B:** 18086/7 (HK-724/5), 18831 (HK-726)

Bahamas World

Formed in March 1968, operations did not begin until 1971 with 707s on inclusive tour charters from Nassau. This business did not prove particularly successful so the airline ceased trading during the summer of 1974.

707-138B: 17700 (VP-BDE). **707-321:** 18084/5 (VP-BDG/F)

Bangladesh Biman
When East Pakistan became the independent State of Bangladesh, it was necessary to set up its own national airline with all speed. The infant country's predicament attracted the sympathy of a number of airlines and governments which led to a motley collection of types joining the newly created Bangladesh Biman. Amongst them was a 707 which was used to introduce the airline's first international charter service between Dhaka and London on 9 March 1972. Thereafter others were received which led to regular scheduled services over a number of routes, although the arrival of DC-10s displaced the 707s from the main sectors. Instead they were transferred to other parts of the network including the Middle and Far East until finally withdrawn in 1989.

707-139B: 17903 (S2-AAL). **707-321C:** 20018 (S2-ACK). **707-331:** 17680 (S2-ABM). **707-349C:** 19354 (S2-ACG). **707-351C:** 18921 (S2-ACF), 19168 (S2-ABN), 19434 (S2-ACA), 19776 (S2-ACE). **707-369C:** 20085 (S2-ACM), **707-373C:** 19441 (S2-ABQ)

Below:
Bangladesh Biman took the Series 351C S2-ACF on strength in August 1980 after service with Cathay Pacific. *AJW*

Above:
Avianca employed this Series 321C as HK-1718 from 1977 until it was disposed of in 1984. *AJW*

Belgian International Air Cargo*
This carrier began non-scheduled cargo operations in the autumn of 1988 using one 707 leased from Okada Air.

707-365C: 19590 (OO-CDE)

Belize Airways
Five 720s were used by the national carrier of Belize for scheduled passenger and cargo services until operations were suspended in 1980. Thereafter the aircraft were stored at Miami.

720-022: 17917 (VP-HCP), 18045 (VP-HCO), 18046 (VP-HCM), 18074 (VP-HCN), 18076 (VP-HCQ)

BEA/British Airtours
Created in 1969 for the purpose of operating IT charter flights, initially ex-BEA Comets were employed. As these became eligible for retirement the company began to receive surplus 707s from BOAC towards the end of 1972. The type then served until the end of the decade and the arrival of new 737s.

707-336B: 20456 (G-AXXY). **707-336C:** 19843 (G-AVPB). **707-436:** 17703 (G-APFB), 17705 (G-APFD), 17707/13 (G-APFF/L), 17716 (G-APFO), 18411 (G-ARRA), 18413 (G-ARRC). **707-465:** 18372 (G-ARWD)

Braniff

One of the first airlines to order the 707, it also became the only customer for the special version designed for use at hot and high altitude airports. Services to South America began in April 1960 although some domestic schedules had been launched just before the previous Christmas. For some years both 707s and 720s were used, but by the early 1970s the routes previously plied had been taken over by DC-8s. For many of the Boeings there was a new, if somewhat more hazardous, career with Trans Mediterranean.

707-138B: 18068/9 (N105BN/6BN), 18739/40 (N107BN/8BN). **707-227:** 17691/5 (N7071/5). **707-327C:** 19104/8 (N7095/9), 19440 (N7100), 19529/31 (N7102/4). **720-022:** 18077 (N7224U). **720-027:** 18064/5 (N7076/7), 18154 (N7078), 18423 (N7079), 18581 (N7080). **720-048:** 18041 (N7083), 18042 (N7081), 18043 (N7082)

Britannia Airways

As the affinity group charter market was flourishing in 1971, it prompted Britannia to enter the long-haul business with a pair of 707s, the first arriving in February. The inaugural flight took place

Below:
After lengthy service on BOAC/British Airways' trunk routes, G-ARRC was transferred to Airtours for IT work in 1976. *AJW*

Bottom:
Delivered in 1967, N7100 only spent four years with Braniff before joining Trans Mediterranean at Beirut. *Sherlock/G. W. Pennick*

Above:
Britannia's association with the 707-373C G-AYSI lasted from February 1971 until April 1973. *AJW*

on 27 April when the 189-seat aircraft visited Tenerife, but normally the destination was the American west coast. Due to increased hostility from the scheduled carriers, the operation of group charters had become more and more difficult by 1973. Since the airline did not wish to become involved in long-haul schedules at that stage, it decided to end this aspect of its activities forthwith. Consequently the two 707s left the fleet for a new life with British Caledonian.

707-355C: 19417 (G-AYEX). **707-373C:** 18707 (G-AYSI)

British Caledonian
See Caledonian Airways

British Eagle
See Cunard Eagle

British Midland Airways
Although essentially a short-haul operator at the time, in 1970 BMA decided to enter the IT market with 707s flying on transatlantic charters. When these became less popular, the airline offered its fleet of aircraft for short or long term leases, particularly to African airlines in the process of starting up. For some years the 707s were to be seen in a variety of liveries, but eventually this activity ended although several were used for European ITs until 1984 when they were withdrawn and sold.

707-321: 17597 (G-AYBJ), 17598 (G-AYVG), 17602 (G-BAEL), 17605 (G-AZWA), 17608 (G-AYXR), 18083 (G-AYVE). **707-321C:** 19270 (N448M/G-BMAZ). **707-324C:** 18886 (G-AZJM). **707-338C:** 19293 (G-BFLE), 19625 (G-BFLD)

Below:
British Midland obtained ex-Qantas 707-338C G-BFLE in 1978 mainly to lease to other operators, but it was later used for IT charters by BMA itself until sold in the US in 1985. *AJW*

British Overseas Airways Corporation/British Airways

After some delays, BOAC was able to introduce its new 707s on to the London-New York route from 6 June 1960 with the Montreal and Toronto service following on 18 August. Gradually the type replaced the Comets and Britannias on the African and Far East runs, although with the delivery of VC10s it was possible to transfer more 707s on to the North Atlantic sectors. In the mid-1960s BOAC received the first of its cargo aircraft, although in reality they were convertible to a passenger configuration. With the arrifval of the 747s in the early 1970s some of the surplus 707s joined British Airtours although British Airways — as the airline became known in 1972 — continued to operate some of the type into the 1980s.

707-336B: 20456/7 (G-AXXY/Z). **707-336C:** 18924/5 (G-ASZF/G), 19498 (G-ATWV), 19843 (G-AVPB), 20374/5 (G-AXGW/X), 20517 (G-AYLT). **707-365C:** 19590 (G-ATZD). **707-379C:** 19821 (G-AWHU). **707-399C:** 19767 (G-AVTW). **707-436:** 17703/17 (G-APFB/P), 18411/3 (G-ARRA/C). **707-465:** 18372/3 (G-ARWD/E)

British West Indian Airways

An extensive network of scheduled passenger and cargo services were operated by the company's 707s taking them to various points in the Caribbean and further afield to New York, Toronto, Guyana and Miami, plus London after April 1974. All of the fleet was acquired secondhand from such as Northwest, Pan American and Braniff, but by 1983 BWIA had replaced the type with TriStars.

707-138B: 18067 (9Y-TDC), 18334 (9Y-TDB). **707-227:** 17692 (9Y-TDO), 17693 (9Y-TDR), 17694/5 (9Y-TDP/Q). **707-321B:** 20027 (9Y-TEX), 20028 (9Y-TEZ). **707-351C:** 19209 (9Y-TED), 19412 (9Y-TEE), 19631/2 (9Y-TEJ/K). **720-048:** 18043 (9Y-TCS)

Above:
One of BOAC's first batch of 707s, G-APFO is seen wearing the carrier's final livery before adopting the British Airways scheme. *AJW*

Burlington Air Express*

This company owns a number of 707s which are used for freight operations over a wide network of routes. All are flown on its behalf by several other carriers such as Orion Air, Southern Air Transport, Rosenbalm and Buffalo Airways.

707-321C: 18766 (N865BX), 19270 (N863BX), 19375 (N864BX). **707-323C:** 19584/5 (N872BX/3BX). **707-338C:** 19293 (N861BX), 19625 (N862BX). **707-399C:** 19415 (N871BX)

Calair Flug

Known until November 1970 as Transportflug, the airline was formed in 1965 to operate passenger and cargo charter flights from Frankfurt. Operations under the new name began in early 1971 using five ex-Eastern 720s. Their new career was shorter than anticipated because the company was forced to suspend its activities in March 1972 and by May it had disappeared completely.

720-025: 18162/3 (D-ACIP/Q), 18240 (D-ACIR), 18242 (D-ACIS), 18244 (D-ACIT)

Caledonian Airways/British Caledonian

From 1961 the airline traded as Caledonian and specialised in passenger and cargo charters particularly across the North Atlantic. When the merger with British United was undertaken in 1970, the newly created British Caledonian inherited a network of scheduled services. This resulted in the existing 707s and others subsequently acquired taking over some of the routes, particularly to West Africa. Although gradually replaced by DC-10s, it was 1984 before the last 707 was retired by BCal.

Above:
For a time after the merger of Caledonian and British United in November 1970, 707-355C G-AXRS carried the combined title as an interim measure. *AJW*

707-323C: 20089 (G-AYZZ). **707-324C:** 18886 (G-AZJM). **707-338C:** 19296 (G-BDEA), 19297 (G-BCAL), 19629/30 (G-BDLM/G-BDSJ). **707-340C:** 20275 (G-AZPW), 20488 (G-AZRO). **707-349C:** 18975 (G-AWTK/G-BDCN), 19354/5 (G-BAWP/G-AWWD). **707-351B:** 18710 (G-BCLZ). **707-355C:** 19664 (G-AXRS), 19417 (G-AYEX). **707-365C:** 19416 (G-ATZC). **707-373C:** 18707 (G-AYSI), **707-399C:** 19415 (G-AVKA), 19767 (G-AVTW). **707-3L6C:** 21096 (G-CDHW)

Cameroon Airlines

After withdrawing its support from the new Air Afrique consortium, Cameroon Airlines was formed to begin operations on 1 November 1971. Passenger services were maintained from Douala to Paris via Rome and Nice with a 707 leased from Air France, but the aircraft was returned to its owner when the carrier received its own specimen from Boeing in 1972.

707-328: 17614 (F-BHSB). **707-3H7C:** 20629 (TJ-CAA)

Canadian Pacific

For a short time during the winter of 1967/68, the Canadian airline operated a 707 on lease due to the late delivery of its DC-8s. Unfortunately the aircraft crashed on 7 February 1968 thereby ending the carrier's brief encounter with the type.

707-138B: 17698 (N791SA)

Cargolux

Although not a dedicated 707 operator, through the years there have been occasions when examples of the type have been leased for short periods when there was a need for greater capacity.

707-331C: 19212 (LX-FCV/LX-BJV). **707-344C:** 19706 (LX-LGT)

Caribbean Air Cargo*

Non-scheduled freight flights are made by this airline to link its Caribbean base with Houston, Miami, New York and San Juan.

707-351C: 19412 (8P-CAC), 19632 (8P-CAD)

Below:
Leased from American Airlines for short periods in 1971 and 1972, this Series 323C was allocated G-AYZZ during its service as a freighter with British Caledonian. *AJW*

Cathay Pacific

Formed in 1946, Cathay Pacific offered a number of local services before later expanding to take in most of the Far East centres. In 1971 the airline began to re-equip with 707s acquired from Northwest and these took over the operation of the route serving Tokyo, Hong Kong, Singapore and Djakarta. By 1976 the fleet numbered 12, but already the first TriStars had arrived. As more of the latter were delivered, so the 707s were withdrawn until finally in 1984 only wide-bodied types were operated.

707-351B: 18584/5 (VR-HGH/I), 18586 (VR-HGO), 18693 (VR-HGN). **707-351C:** 18747/8 (VR-HHB/HD), 18888/9 (VR-HHE/HJ), 18921/2 (VR-HGR/P), 18964 (VR-HGQ), 19034 (VR-HGU)

Challenge Air Cargo*

This is a relatively new Miami-based airline formed in 1986 to provide both scheduled and charter cargo flights between the Florida airport, Colombia, Panama, Costa Rica, Peru and Paraguay.

707-323C: 19582 (N8402). **707-327C:** 19529 (N707AD). **707-330C:** 20124 (N707HE)

China Airlines

As the national carrier of Taiwan, in 1970 China Airlines introduced its 707s to the long-haul links between Taipei and the American west coast calling at such centres as Tokyo, Honolulu, Hong Kong and Osaka. Although reduced in numbers, the type remained in use until the mid-1980s but mainly for cargo work.

707-309C: 20261/2 (B-1824/26). **707-321C:** 18825 (B-1832). **707-324C:** 18887 (B-1834), 19178 (B-1830). **707-351B:** 18710 (B-1828)

China Southwest Airways*

See CAAC

Civil Aviation Administration of China (CAAC)*

Unlike Taiwan's national carrier, CAAC was a late customer for the 707 when ordering a batch of 10 for deliveries spread between August 1973 and May 1974. It followed a more relaxed policy with the outside world and the aircraft were used to introduce routes to European and North American centres in addiiton to others in the Far East. Some of the 707s had been transferred to the new China Southwest Airways by 1988.

707-3J6B: 20714/7 (B-2402/4/6/8). **707-3J6C:** 20718/23 (B-2410/12/14/16/18/20)

Compania Dominicana de Aviacion*

Although 727s have maintained most of the carrier's schedules, a pair of 707s were leased from Pan American in 1972 while delivery of the trijets was awaited. Some years later another specimen was taken on strength for use on the longer stages.

707-321: 17604 (N726PA), 17689 (N706PA). **707-399C:** 19767 (HI-442CT)

Conair

Since its launch in 1965, Conair has always been involved in IT charter work from Denmark to various holiday areas in Europe. At first five DC-7s were employed, but these were replaced in 1971

Below:
Challenge Air Cargo uses this one-time American Airlines Series 323C N8402 for its regular cargo flights into Miami. *A. S. Wright*

by five ex-Eastern 720s. The last of this batch was
withdrawn in 1981, but the airline continued with
the type by acquiring Maersk's fleet when the latter
began to receive its 737s. It was not until 1987 that
the surviving 720s were finally withdrawn and their
duties taken over by three Airbus A300s.

720-025: 18157/59/61 (OY-DSK/L/M), 18241/43
(OY-DSP/R). **720-051B:** 18384 (OY-APZ),
18421/2 (OY-APY/PW), 18792/3 (OY-APU/V)

Condor Flugdienst
This Lufthansa subsidiary operated several 707s
which were leased from the parent company. They
were generally used for IT charter work to the
Mediterranean and Canary Islands, but by the early
1980s the type had been phased out in favour of
727s, 737s and DC-10s.

707-330B: 18462 (D-ABOV), 18928/9
(D-ABUF/G), 19315/6 (D-ABUL/M), 20123
(D-ABUJ). **707-430:** 17718/9 (D-ABOB/C), 17721
(D-ABOF)

Continental Airlines
Along with Pan American and Braniff, Continental
was one of the first customers for the 707 when it
ordered four Series 120s in December 1955. By
1969 the early version had been replaced by the
longer-range Series 320 which the carrier needed
to fulfil its military charter obligations. They were
also employed on new scheduled services including
Los Angeles-Honolulu and other long-distance
sectors. However, by the mid-1970s all the 707s
and 720s had left the airline.

707-124: 17609/11 (N70773/5), 17612 (N70785),
18012 (N74612). **707-321C:** 18825/6 (N17321/2).
707-324C: 18886/7 (N17323/4), 19177/8
(N17325/6), 19350/2 (N17327/9), 19353
(N47330), 19869/70 (N47331/2), 19871 (N67333).
720-024B: 18416/9 (N57201/4), 18587 (N57205),
18763 (N57206), 19002/3 (N17207/8)

Cunard Eagle/British Eagle
As a result of a partnership between Eagle and
Cunard, this airline was set up in 1960 to operate
services to Bermuda from the UK and US. When
the first 707 was delivered in 1962 it was registered
on the island and used on the New York route. A
service originating in London was extended to
Miami to provide a through facility for those
travelling to Florida. However, it was not long
before Cunard changed its partner to establish
BOAC-Cunard while Eagle added British to its title
to become independent once again. Subsequently
a pair of ex-Qantas 707s were used on long-haul
charters until 1968 when the company went into
liquidation.

707-138B: 17699 (G-AVZZ), 17702 (G-AWDG).
707-365C: 19416 (G-ATZC — not delivered),
19590 (G-ATZD). **707-465:** 18372 (VR-BBW/
G-ARWD), 18373 (G-ARWE)

Cyprus Airways
Prior to 1974 Cyprus Airways was building up its
scheduled network and was linking the island with
major cities in Europe and the Middle East.
Operations were rudely interrupted by the arrival of
hostile Turks which led to the destruction of most of
the airline's fleet. When common sense began to
prevail once again, operations were resumed and in
due course a number of 707s were introduced.
Even with the arrival of Airbus A310s in the
mid-1980s, the older machines continued to serve
on the thinner routes and for IT flights.

707-123B: 17628 (5B-DAM), 17631/2
(5B-DAL/K), 17635 (5B-DAP), 18054 (5B-DAO)

Dairo Air Service*

Operating as DAS Air Cargo, the Uganda company was formed to provide scheduled and charter freight services between Africa and Europe.

707-321B: 18832 (5X-JCR). **707-321C:** 18825 (5X-DAR). **707-338C:** 18809 (5N-ARQ)

Dan-Air Services

In 1970 Dan-Air was granted permission to operate transatlantic charters for an initial period of five years. An ex-Pan American 707 was handed over on 7 January 1971 and after a sesson of crew training, was ready to enter service towards the end of March. For its first season G-AYSL was used mainly for group affinity charters to the US on behalf of CPS Jetsave, but during the peak months it was to be found on some of the airline's busier European IT routes. A second 707 joined Dan-Air in time for the next summer season and others were operated as freighters for IAS Cargo. All 707s had been withdrawn by the end of the 1970s either to be scrapped or passed on to other carriers.

707-321: 17599/600 (G-AYSL/G-AZTG). **707-321C:** 18579 (G-BEBP), 18591 (G-BEAF), 18765 (G-BEZT), 19271 (G-BEVN)

DETA Mozambique Airlines

Prior to 1976 the airline operated domestic schedules plus regular visits to neighbouring countries. DETA's first intercontinental route was

Below:
Dan-Air's first 707 was the Series 321 G-AYSL.
AJW

launched at the beginning of the year with 707s leased from the UK company Tempair. This venture linked Luanda with Lisbon, but at the end of the summer the service was dropped and the aircraft returned to whence they came.

707-321: 17593 (9G-ACB/C9-ARF), 17603 (9G-ACD), 18013 (C9-ARG)

Donaldson International

Although formed in 1964, it was five years before the airline began operations in its own right with three Britannias. Due to the popularity of its transatlantic charter flights, Donaldson expanded its fleet at the end of 1970 with the aid of a pair of ex-Pan American 707s, the first entering service on 20 May 1971. They were principally employed for IT work from Glasgow, but their other duties also frequently took them to North America having generally replaced the Britannias on the Atlantic run. There was also a demand for long-haul charters to the Far East, so two additional 707s were acquired during 1972 to provide the extra capacity. Following infringements of the group charter regulations, Donaldson's operations were severely affected and two of the aircraft had to be sold in order to raise sufficient capital to meet the CAA's new requirements. A reduced number of ITs were flown during 1973, but 1974 was to be the last year of operation despite a contract to operate two 707s for Iraqi Airlines and a third converted for freight work. On 8 August all flying ceased and the aircraft returned to Pan American.

707-321: 17598 (G-AYVG), 17602 (G-BAEL), 17605 (G-AZWA), 17608 (G-AYXR)

Eagle Air

This Icelandic company began charter operations in 1978 with a pair of 720s from the defunct Air Viking. In addition to their normal work, the aircraft frequently found themselves on lengthy leases to other carriers. To cover such absences a 707 joined the fleet in 1980, but in the following year it was returned to Western Airlines. Several others were obtained both for leases and flying on Eagle Air's own charters, but the last finally left in 1986.

707-321C: 19270 (TF-VLL). **707-324C:** 19351 (TF-VLJ). **707-347C:** 19964 (TF-VLG). **707-382B:** 18962 (TF-VLV). **720-025:** 18163 (TF-VLA). **720-047B:** 18820 (TF-VLC), 18827 (TF-VLB)

Eastern Air Lines

Eastern opted for the DC-8 when selecting a type for its long routes, but ordered a number of 720s which it considered more suitable for its short-range services. Deliveries began in August 1961 and was completed early in the New Year. Unlike most 720s, none of the batch were ever converted to the more popular B standard. During 1969/70 Eastern returned all aircraft to the manufacturer in part-exchange for 727s.

720-025: 18155/64 (N8701E/10E), 18240/4 (N8711E/5E)

Ecuatoriana*

As the national airline of Ecuador from 1974, the carrier began scheduled services to a variety of destinations in the Americas for which purpose it obtained a pair of 720s from Israel Aircraft Industries. Several years later 707s were added to the fleet.

707-321B: 19265 (HC-BCT), 19277 (HC-BFC), 20033 (HC-BHY). **707-321C:** 19273 (HC-BGP). **720-023B:** 18033 (HC-BDP), 18036/7 (HC-AZP/Q)

Egyptair/United Arab Airlines*

Four 707s were ordered by UAA in 1966 for use on the airline's proposed transatlantic services. However, when the aircraft were delivered in 1968 it was decided that it would be more useful if they replaced the Comets currently maintaining the European schedules. The new arrivals therefore took over the London run and their presence also allowed the carrier to resurrect the Cairo-Hong Kong-Tokyo route in 1969. Known as Egyptair after 10 October 1971, the company continued to employ the 707s and in fact was amongst the last commercial operators to order the type in the mid-1970s.

707-366C: 19844/5 (SU-AOU/OW), 20341/2 (SU-APD/E), 20760/2 (SU-AVX/Z), 20673 (SU-AXA), 20920 (SU-AXK)

El Al/Arkia*

Eager to join the jet age, El Al managed to lease a 707 so that it could begin a link between Tel Aviv and New York in January 1961. With the arrival of its own aircraft later that year, the airline was able to introduce a non-stop schedule over the route which, at 5,000 miles, was one of the longest flown at the time. Two 720s were delivered in the spring of 1962 for use on the shorter sectors in Africa and the Middle East, although occasionally circumstances necessitated their employment on the Atlantic services. With the arrival of 747s, the 707s were increasingly used for charter work with a 187-seat tourist cabin for both Arkia and Sun d'Or.

707-349C: 19354/5 (N324F/5F). **707-358B:** 19004 (4X-ATR), 19502 (4X-ATS), 20097 (4X-ATT). **707-358C:** 20122 (4X-ATX), 20301 (4X-ATY). **707-441:** 17906 (PP-VJB). **707-458:** 18070/1 (4X-ATA/B), 18357 (4X-ATC). **720-048:** 18041 (EI-ALA). **720-058B:** 18424/5 (4X-ABA/B)

Ethiopian Airlines

Ethiopean's first jet airliners were two 720s for use on the airline's Nairobi and Madrid schedules commencing in January 1963. Other routes gradually became the responsibility of the aircraft until two 707s arrived in May 1968. Together with other 720s subsequently acquired, they served until

the mid-1980s although one 707 was lost in 1977. When the 720s were finally withdrawn they had the satisfaction of knowing that some of their vital parts were to sustain USAF KC-135s.

707-327C: 19531 (ET-AIV). **707-360C:** 19736 (ET-ACD). **707-379C:** 19820 (ET-ACQ). **720-024B:** 18417 (ET-AFK), 18418/9 (ET-AFA/B). **720-060B:** 18454/5 (ET-AAG/H), 18977 (ET-ABP)

Fast Air Carrier*

This Chilian cargo carrier has used the 707 for a series of cargo flights between its homeland and points in North and South America since operations began in 1978.

707-331C: 19435 (CC-CAF), 20069 (CC-CUE)

Florida West Airlines*

Cargo and charter services are flown from Miami to various points in the Caribbean and Central America.

707-321C: 20017 (N710FW). **707-331C:** 18711 (N700FW), 19212 (N730FW). **707-351C:** 19263 (N720FW), 19411 (N740FW)

Flying Tiger Line

Use of the 707 by Flying Tiger was limited to a few years in the mid-1960s when there was a need for a more modern type to replace older generation aircraft. For a time the majority were employed on military charter work, but gradually the machines were either returned to their owners or leased to other carriers.

707-348C: 18880 (N318F). **707-349C:** 18975/6 (N322F/3F), 19354/5 (N324F/5F). **707-358B:** 19004 (N317F). **707-399C:** 19415 (N319F)

GAS Air Cargo*
Operating from Lagos, the carrier is mainly involved in freight charter work with its 707s which are operated on its behalf by Dairo Air Service. A scheduled service is operated from Entebbe to Europe.

707-321C: 19372 (5N-AWO). **707-338C:** 18809 (5N-ARQ). **707-351C:** 19168 (5N-AYJ)

German Cargo Services
Lufthansa set up this subsidiary so that domestic and international cargo services could be operated between Germany, the Near East and both East and West Africa. Two 707s were transferred from the parent company for activities to start in 1977, to be followed by two more over the next two years. During 1984 the airline disposed of its entire fleet in favour of DC-8-73s.

Above:
New in 1966, the 707-358B 4X-ATR entered service with El Al although it has operated for both Sun D'Or and Arkia at times. *AJW*

707-330C: 18932 (D-ABUE), 18937 (D-ABUA), 19371 (D-ABUI), 20124 (D-ABUO)

Geminair
In 1977 Geminair acquired a 707 from Lufthansa to use on its regular cargo runs to London, Frankfurt and Paris from its base at Accra, Ghana. After a period of reorganisation in the early 1980s the airline disposed of its aircraft but used a 707 of Tradewinds and later Anglo Cargo as required.

707-430: 17721 (9G-ACK)

Below:
Florida West registered this Series 321C as N710FW when it took delivery in 1986. *A. S. Wright*

Global International Airways

Passenger charters began with 707s in August 1978 and were operated from Detroit to Hawaii, Las Vegas, Europe and the Caribbean. Long-haul cargo flights were also undertaken especially between South America and Miami. There were no further services after December 1983 when its operating certificate was withdrawn following financial trouble.

707-321B: 19695 (N498GA), 19697 (N495PA), 20020 (N881PA), 20026 (N887PA/N160GL). **707-323B:** 19588/9 (N8409/10), 20172 (N8433/N161GL), 20176 (N8437), 20179 (N8440). **707-323C:** 20087 (N8415), 20089 (N8417/N162GL)

Guy-America Airways/American Overseas

Operations commenced on 2 June 1981 for the purpose of offering scheduled services between New York and Georgetown, Guyana, using a fleet of 707s. Worldwide charter flights were operated under the name of American Overseas Airways, but all activity ceased in March 1983 coincident with the suspension of the airline's certificate.

707-123B: 17646 (N519GA), 19333 (N7583A). **707-321B:** 18840 (N707GE), 19695 (N498GA), 20032 (N895PA)

Above:
In the late 1970s/early 1980s the 707s of Global International were regularly seen around the world during the course of their charter duties. When photographed in 1982 this -321B still carried its Pan American registration, N887PA, but subsequently it adopted the new identity, N160GL. *AJW*

Guyana Airways*

The present name was adopted in 1963 when a comprehensive network of scheduled services was introduced. From the early 1980s a 707 has been leased from time to time for use on the carrier's longer-haul routes.

707-321B: 19693 (N1181Z), 20019 (N880PA), 20034 (N732Q)

Hang Khong Vietnam*

Most of the equipment used by this carrier is of Russian origin, but several 707s have been employed for longer sectors since the start-up in 1978. All services are confined to the Far East area at present.

707-321B: 18832 (VN-A305/VN-81416). **707-344:** 17929 (VN-304). **707-379C:** 19821 (VN-83415)

HeavyLift Cargo Airlines*

After nine years as an airline specialising in the movement of outsize loads, in March 1989 HeavyLift expanded its coverage to include normal palletised cargo. To cater for this business a 707 was acquired, the first jet to be operated by the UK carrier. Such was its success that a second was leased during the year, while a UK registered machine was expected in 1990.

707-323C: 18940 (N108BV). **707-351C:** 19631 (N2215Y)

Hispaniola Airways

This Dominican Republic airline was created in 1981 to operate cargo services between Santo Domingo and Miami, always a popular airport for such traffic. Passenger flights were also planned to link Puerto Plata with the Florida city and New York. A 707 and a 720 made up the fleet, but the former was withdrawn at the end of 1981 and quietly allowed to rot away at Miami. Its companion was also retired in 1983 and thereafter the airline leased a 727 for its operations.

707-124: 17610 (HI-384). **720-022:** 18049 (N421MA/HI-401)

IAS Cargo Airlines

Although essentially a DC-8 operator, IAS leased two 707s from Dan-Air in 1976 for use on its African services. Unfortunately one of the aircraft was lost in 1977 so another took its place until the contract ended in 1978. In 1979, IAS was renamed British Cargo Airlines and became a CL-44/DC-8 operator.

707-321C: 18579 (G-BEBP), 18591 (G-BEAF), 18717 (G-BGIS), 19271 (G-BEVN)

Independent Air/Atlanta Skylarks*

Established in 1966, this airline has always been involved in charter services. A 720 was introduced in 1973 which then handled the traffic until it was joined by another in 1981. In the mid-1980s the expanding carrier adopted its parent company's Independent Air title which was then carried on the 707s newly acquired for international flights.

707-321B: 20025 (N728Q). **707-331B:** 19570 (N7232X), 19572 (N7231T). **720-022:** 18081 (N7228U). **720-025:** 18159 (N7229L)

InterAm

See Sunrise Airlines

Below:
The 707-351C N2215Y joined HeavyLift for a one year lease on 1 March 1989. *HeavyLift*

Intercontinental Airlines
Most of the carrier's activities are carried out in Africa, but occasional sorties are made to Europe, especially the UK. While DC-8s were normally used for long sectors, a 707 was employed during 1979 for passenger charters and another was operated by the carrier as a freighter in 1983.

707-321C: 19377 (EL-AJA). **707-328** 17921 (N90287)

Inter Frêt Transport Aérien/Air Region*
Both domestic and regional passenger and cargo services were provided by this carrier after it was formed in 1979. A 707 joined the airline in 1981 with a second arriving in 1983, both serving until the carrier was merged with Air Charter Service and the aircraft taken over by Air Region in 1985.

707-321: 17602 (9Q-CZK). **707-344:** 17930 (9Q-CZF)

International Air Bahama
This airline started operations on 20 July 1968 when it introduced low-cost services between Nassau and Luxembourg. As a major shareholder in the company, Executive Jet Aviation supplied a 707 for the venture, but in October 1969 IAB was taken over by the Icelandic carrier, Loftleidir. As a result the latter substituted one of its DC-8s for the 707 which was returned to its owner.

707-355C: 19417 (N525EJ)

International Caribbean Airways
Operations began in December 1970 to feature a low-fare scheduled run between Luxembourg and Barbados with the Gatwick sector added one year later. Closely associated with Laker Airways, ICA used one of the latter's 707s for its services. The airline's title was amended in 1975 with the word 'International' dropped and in due course the 707 was replaced by Laker DC-10s as required.

707-138B: 17699 (G-AVZZ)

Invicta International
After several periods of inactivity, Invicta International was re-formed in 1970 to provide IT charter flights with Vanguards operating mainly from Manston and Luton. In 1974 the company moved into the jet age with a pair of ex-American Airlines' 720s, but most of their time was spent on lease during the two years or so with Invicta. With their departure in 1976 the company reverted to all cargo work this time with Britannias.

707-023: 18013/4 (G-BCBB/A)

Iran Air*
Formed at the beginning of 1962, Iran Air ordered its first 707s in December 1968. Scheduled services with the new aircraft were started on the carrier's European routes in early 1970. Inevitably they were replaced on the trunk routes by later types and relegated either to regional services, pilgrim flights or freight work.

707-321B: 18958 (EP-IRJ). **707-321C:** 19267 (EP-IRK). **707-386C:** 20287/8 (EP-IRL/M), 20741 (EP-IRN).

Iraqi Airways*
It was 1974 before Iraqi Airways purchased three 707s from Boeing although many years earlier a provisional order for two 720s had been placed but was not finalised. The carrier has used the 707s for schedules to other Middle East countries although one was converted into a freighter in 1982 for the use of Arab Air Cargo.

707-370C: 20889/91 (YI-AGE/G)

Jamahiriya Air Transport/ United African Airlines
Formed in 1982, the carrier began operating domestic and international passenger and cargo charter flights mostly to centres within the confines of Africa or to Eastern Europe. A ready-made fleet of 707s was gained in 1983 when the assets of the four-year-old United African Airlines were taken over, but in 1987 Jamahiriya itself was integrated into Libyan Arab Airlines.

707-123B: 17647 (5A-DHM). **707-321C:** 18765 (5A-DHL). **707-338C:** 18955 (5A-DJO). **707-348C:** 18880 (5A-DIX), 19001 (5A-DIY). **707-351C:** 18746 (5A-DIZ), 18888/9 (5A-DJS/T), 18964 (5A-DJU). **707-365C:** 19590 (5A-DJV)

Japan Air Lines (JAL)
When the time came to order jets for its long-haul services, JAL chose the DC-8, but the airline was anxious to start a polar route between Tokyo and Paris as early as possible. Accordingly, it entered into an agreement with Air France whereby the latter supplied 707s for jointly operated services commencing in 1960. Several of the aircraft were repainted to reflect both carriers' colour schemes, but JAL withdrew from the partnership in June 1961 when it had received sufficient DC-8s to maintain its own operation.

707-328: 17613 (F-BHSA), 17617/8 (F-BHSE/F)

Jugoslav Airlines (JAT)*
When JAT received its first secondhand 707 in 1970 it entered service on the airline's main

Above:
JAT acquired the 707-340C YU-AGG from Pakistan International in 1972. *AJW*

European routes. Later the type took over the Middle and Far East schedules as the network was expanded, while it was not unknown for a 707 to be found on peak time domestic runs. As the fleet was reduced in size, so the survivors were used for IT charters or converted for cargo work.

707-321: 17594 (YU-AGH), 17600 (N722PA), 17601 (YU-AGA), 17602 (N724PA). **707-340C:** 19284/6 (YU-AGE/G/F), 19866 (YU-AGD). **707-351C:** 19210 (YU-AGI), 19411 (YU-AGJ)

Katale Aero Transport*
Most of the airline's income is derived from the movement of coffee with its cargo fleet, one 707 being included in the total.

707-329C: 19162 (9Q-CVG)

Kenya Airways*
When East African Airways ceased operations the Kenyan government quickly formed its own national carrier to continue the scheduled services to Europe, the Middle East and India. Three 707s were purchased from Northwest and these were joined during the next year by an ex-Western 720. These have continued in service despite the arrival of a pair of Airbus A310s.

707-351B: 19633/4 (5Y-BBJ/I), 19872 (5Y-BBK). **720-047B:** 18588 (5Y-BBX)

Korean Air Lines/Korean Air*
In 1969 Korean took delivery of a pair of ex-Eastern 720s for use on regional services from Seoul. Next to appear was a brand new 707 which was earmarked for the carrier's schedule to Honolulu and Los Angeles. This aircraft was joined by others of the type, but all future examples were secondhand. Eventually several were modified for freight work but even this activity has been virtually taken over by Airbus A300s on normal passenger duties.

707-321B: 18337 (HL7430), 19363 (HL7429), 19366 (HL7435). **707-321C:** 19369 (HL7431), 19372 (HL7427). **707-338C:** 19626 (HL7432), 19628 (HL7433). **707-373C:** 19715/6 (HL7412/25). **707-3B5C:** 20522 (HL7406)

Kuwait Airways
When the airline decided to replace both its Comets and Tridents it chose the 707 to eventually take over all of its operations. Three were delivered in November 1968 followed just over three years later by another pair. Together the five were flown from Kuwait to most Middle East capitals and to London, the latter trip also including stops at Athens, Rome, Geneva, Frankfurt and Paris en route. Three secondhand specimens joined the company in the mid-1970s, but 10 years later the airline had disposed of the entire fleet.

707-311C: 19789 (9K-ACX). **707-321C:** 20016 (9K-ACS), 20018 (9K-ACU). **707-369C:** 20084/6 (9K-ACJ/L), 20546/7 (9K-ACM/N)

LAC Colombia
Cargo services are operated from Colombia to Florida, Panama and Venezuela in addition to those within South America. Its fleet included DC-8s and a leased 707, but the latter was returned to its owner in 1989.

707-311C: 19789 (N524SJ)

Laker Airways
After a Britannia operated Laker's first commercial flight on 29 July 1966, the airline steadily expanded until by 1969 it was able to acquire the two 707s made available by the demise of British Eagle. The pair were not only used for transatlantic charters, but also for European ITs for a variety of British airports. In 1970 one of the aircraft was used by the associate company, International Caribbean,

Below:
Leased from Southern Air Transport, this 707-311C was operated as N524SJ by LAC Colombia.
A. S. Wright

Bottom:
Caribbean Airways flights were operated by Laker's 707s, in this case the Series 351B, G-BFBS. *AJW*

although when not required by this company it filled in its time with Laker. Daily, low-cost, no-reservation transatlantic scheduled services were proposed in 1971 using DC-10s in the peak times supported by the 707s in less busy periods. It took years to gain approval, but when eventually it was received, the 707s were still in service although both were sold before the collapse of the airline in 1982.

707-138B: 17699 (G-AVZZ), 17702 (G-AWDG)

LAN-Chile*
A large network already existed when the airline acquired its first 707 to fulfil an ambition to expand its coverage to Europe. Lufthansa was the source but a change of plan found the aircraft used to extend its Miami service on to New York. In due course the original plan came to fruition as more 707s were obtained to enable Frankfurt, Madrid and Paris to be served.

707-321B: 19374 (CC-CEK), 19693 (CC-CEJ), 20021 (CC-CEI). **707-330B:** 18462 (CC-CCG), 18926 (CC-CEA). **707-351B:** 18584 (CC-CCX. **707-351C:** 19443 (CC-CCK). **707-385C:** 19000 (CC-CEB)

Above:
A fairly late machine delivered in 1976, 5A-DAK is used for VIP work with Libyan Arab. *Boeing*

Liberia World Airlines
For a time in the early 1980s Liberia's 707 roamed the world on freight charters or on temporary detachment to other operators.

707-321C: 19377 (EL-AIY/EL-AJA). **707-330B:** 19315 (EL-AJU)

Libyan Arab Airlines*
Following a national revolution on 1 September 1969, the Libyan national carrier assumed the present title by dropping all references to a kingdom. With the exception of a 707 operated as a VIP transport, the airline did not possess any of the type until the early 1980s although a number were

also leased in this period. The situation changed in 1987 however because it inherited the fleet of Jamahiriya when the latter company was integrated.

707-321B: 19378 (5A-DJM). **707-321C:** 18765 (5A-DHL). **707-324C:** 19351 (TF-VLJ). **707-328B:** 18686 (5A-DLT). **707-328C:** 18881 (5A-DIK). **707-348C:** 18880 (5A-DIX), 19001 (5A-DIY). **707-349C:** 19354 (EI-ASO). **707-351C:** 18888/9 (5A-DJT/U)

Lloyd Aeroo Boliviano*
An airline with a long history dating back to 1925, LAB acquired its first 707 in 1977 for use on its cargo services. A passenger version was added in 1981 which was then employed on the busier sectors such as Miami, although by 1987 this specimen had also been converted for freight work.

707-323C: 18692 (CP-1365), 19586 (CP-1698)

Above:
Stansted-based Lloyd International obtained the 707-324C G-AZJM in 1971 for use on long-haul charter work. *Wegg/G. W. Pennick*

Lloyd International

In April 1970 Lloyd took delivery of a 189-seat 707 to complement its Britannias. For most of the first season the aircraft flew charters to the Far East and the US from its base at Stansted. A second 707 was delivered in February 1971 and together the two were fully occupied with transatlantic group affinity charters throughout the summer. At the end of the year a third machine was added to the fleet, but although the US business kept the company employed, the rewards were small. In an effort to survive, one of the 707s was leased to El Al but

Below:
The 720 had a relatively short career with Lufthansa, D-ABOH being the first to be delivered in 1961. Three years later it and others of the type were sold to Pan American. *Boeing*

before the aircraft left for Tel Aviv, Lloyd was forced to cease all operations in June 1972.

707-321: 18084 (G-AYRZ), 18085 (G-AYAG).
707-324C: 18886 (G-AZJM)

Lufthansa

The German flag carrier was able to begin modernising its long-haul fleet in 1960. Both New York and Chicago were linked with Hamburg and Frankfurt during the year, while 1961 saw the first of the 720s operating on the Middle East and South American routes. Throughout the 1960s the network was expanded as new and longer range 707s were taken on strength, the type remaining the airline's mainstay for its intercontinental services until the arrival of the early 747s at the end of 1970. Nevertheless it was the mid-1980s before the last left the airline having generally spent the final years employed on charter work. On the other hand the 720s did not have a long career with Lufthansa since by 1966 the survivors had been sold.

707-330B: 18462/3 (D-ABOV/T), 18819 (D-ABOX), 18923 (D-ABUB), 18926/31

(D-ABUC/D/F/G/H/K), 19315/6 (D-ABUL/M).
707-330C: 18932 (D-ABUE), 18937 (D-ABUA),
19317 (D-ABUI), 20123/4 (D-ABUJ/O), 20395
(D-ABUY). **707-430:** 17718/21 (D-ABOB/C/D/F),
18056 (D-ABOG). **720-030B:** 18057/60
(D-ABOH/K/L/M), 18248/51 (D-ABON/P/Q/R)

Luxair/Trek Airways

Trek became the designated airline to operate
between Johannesburg and Luxembourg on a
weekly basis with two 707s from 1969. Both were
registered in the European country and carried
Luxair livery in order to forestall any demonstrations from those unsympathetic to South African
policies. When Trek ceased trading in 1976, the two
aircraft were sold but others were acquired by
Luxair mainly for its IT programme to the
Mediterranean and Canary Islands. By 1985 this
activity had been completely taken over by 737s
and an Airbus A300.

707-344: 17930 (LX-LGW). **707-344B:** 18891
(LX-LGR), 19133 (LX-LGU). **707-344C:** 19706
(LX-LGT), 20283 (LX-LGS). **707-348C:** 18737
(LX-LGV)

Above:
**A number of 707s have been used by Luxair,
LX-LGV originally being one of the Aer Lingus
fleet.** *Liam Byrne*

Maersk

Since it was formed in 1969, Maersk has always
been active in the IT and charter market. In 1973
the first of a fleet of 720s arrived at the airline's
Copenhagen base to be joined at intervals by
another four. These then flew on the popular
holiday routes to the UK and Mediterranean area
for some years before being eventually replaced by
737s. In 1981 they were sold to Conair, another
Danish carrier engaged in the same type of
business.

720-051B: 18394 (OY-APZ), 18421/2 (OY-A-
PY/W), 18792/3 (OY-APU/V)

Below:
**Maersk acquired this 720 from Northwest in 1974
although until the end of the following year it was
leased to Monarch. Registered OY-APU, the aircraft
was operated by the Danish carrier until sold to
Conair in 1981.** *AJW*

Above:
In the early 1980s, the 720 4X-BMA was one of a pair operated by the Israeli charter carrier Maof. *AJW*

Malaysia-Singapore Airlines/Singapore International Airlines

Previously known as Malaysian Airways, the airline was formed in 1947. A comprehensive route network was built up to neighbouring countries, from 1970 using 707s to replace Comets on the Singapore-Kuala Lumpur-Colombo-Madras schedule. As more aircraft became available the Perth/Melbourne route was taken over while the

Below:
Middle East Airlines has operated the 707 and 720 for over 20 years with little prospect of more modern equipment replacing the veterans. Both types are used on schedules, in this case flown by the ex-American Airlines 720-023B OD-AFM. *AJW*

London service became the preserve of the 707s on 2 June 1971. In the following year the airline was split into Malaysian Airlines System and Singapore Airlines following the withdrawal of Malaysia from the consortium. All the 707s were transferred to SIA and continued in service until the early 1980s.

707-312B: 19737/9 (9V-BBA/9M-AOT/9V-BBB). **707-324C:** 19351/3 (9V-BEW/Y). **707-327C:** 19529/30 (9M-AQB/9V-BDC). 9M-AOT/9M-AQB were reregistered 9V-BFB/C with SIA. The latter also acquired **707-338C:** 18808/9 (9V-BFW/N)

Malaysian Airlines System
After the split with Singapore, MAS inaugurated its own long-haul routes which were flown by some ex-Qantas 707s. These continued in service until finally replaced in the early 1980s.

707-338C: 18953/5 (9M-ASQ/9M-ATR/9M-ASO later 9M-MCQ/R/S)

Maof Airlines

Elevated from an Israeli general aviation operator in 1969 to an IT carrier in 1981, Maof started its operations with two 720s. During its lifetime the charter flights took the airline to a dozen or so different European airports, but in late 1984 operations ceased because of financial losses.

707-139B: 17903 (N778PA). **707-331B:** 19226 (N18712). **707-336B:** 20456 (4X-BMC). **707-023B:** 18013/4 (4X-BMB/A)

Merpati Nusantara

One 707 was employed by the Indonesian airline to operate IT flights between Jakarta and Manila in the Philippines. Leased from July 1976 until 1979, ownership then passed to the carrier but the aircraft was withdrawn in 1981.

707-138B: (N109BN/PK-MBA)

Middle East Airlines*

After leasing a 720 for several years MEA finally managed to place an order for four new 707s, the first two being delivered towards the end of 1968. One had the misfortune of being destroyed after only one month, the result of some organised destruction by a band of Israelis. Through the years the airline has therefore operated a number of 707/720s, many of which have suffered at the hands of those determined to continue the local unrest. Not surprisingly MEA has not found it easy to replace the aircraft with a more modern type, so the elderly machines still continue to faithfully maintain the airline's services.

707-323C: 19515/6 (OD-AHD/E), 19588/9 (OD-AHB/C). **707-347C:** 19966/7 (OD-AGU/V). **707-3B4C:** 20224/5 (OD-AFB/C), 20259/60 (OD-AFD/E). **720-023B:** 18017 (OD-AFP), 18018/20 (OD-AFR/T), 18021 (OD-AGB), 18024 (OD-AFQ), 18025 (OD-AFZ), 18026 (OD-AFW), 18027 (OD-AFM), 18029 (OD-AFU), 18030 (OD-AFN), 18034 (OD-AFL), 18035 (OD-AFO). **720-047B:** 18828 (OD-AGG), 18830 (OD-AGF), 18963 (OD-AGE), 19160/1 (OD-AGQ/R)

Millon Air*

See Pan Aviation

Misr Overseas Airways

This title was adopted in October 1983 when passenger and cargo charter services were begun from its Cairo base. Previously the company was known as Air Lease Egypt and was not involved in operations. Subsequently the airline expanded its coverage to include Africa, Asia, Europe and Latin America, but ceased flying in late 1989.

707-138B: 18068/9 (SU-FAB/A). **707-323C:** 20087 (SU-FAC). **707-351C:** 19775 (SU-EAA)

Monarch Airlines

For the first few years of its existence, Monarch operated a number of Britannias for its IT charter flights. By the early 1970s the time was approach-

Below:
Monarch normally used its 720Bs for IT work, but on this occasion G-AZNX was chartered by P&O for a 30-day Round-The-World Air Holiday. *P&O Cruises*

ing when they needed to be replaced, so three ex-Northwest 720s were acquired, all entering service by April 1972. Such was the volume of traffic achieved on flights to the Mediterranean area and the Canary Islands that during the remainder of the 1970s additional 720s and two 707s were leased for varying periods. By 1981 Monarch was only operating two examples of the former type, but these remained on strength until 1983 when the arrival of 757s ended their careers in the UK.

707-123B: 17632 (G-BFMI), 18054 (G-BGCT). **720-023B:** 18013/4 (G-BCBB/A). **720-051B:** 18381/3 (G-AZFB/ZKM/ZNX), 18421 (G-BHGE), 18792 (G-BBZG)

Montana
Based at Klagenfurt, Austria, Montana was formed in 1975 to undertake worldwide passenger and freight charters, although these tended to be seasonal links between Vienna, American centres and the Far East. Its 707s were also used by other carriers on a subcontract basis, but the income was insufficient to prevent Montana becoming insolvent in July 1981.

707-138B: 18068 (OE-IRA), 18069 (OE-INA). **707-396C:** 20043 (OE-IDA)

Naganagani*
Registered in Upper Volta, this company operates non-scheduled flights with 707s in association with the French airline, Point Air.

707-321B: 18837 (XT-ABY). **707-336C:** 18925 (XT-ABX), **707-328C:** 19521 (XT-BBF)

NATO*
Deliveries of the NATO-operated AWACS aircraft began in 1981 and continued until 1985. The three Series 329Cs were acquired from Sabena in 1986 for training purposes.

707-329C: 19996 (LX-N19996), 20198 (LX-N20198), 20199 (LX-N20199). **E-3A:** 22838/22854 (LX-N90443/LX-90459), 22855 (LX-N90442)

Nigeria Airways*
After leasing a 707 for several years in the 1960s, Nigeria Airways was eventually able to purchase its own machine from Boeing. When completed by the manufacturer in 1970 it was to be another year before it was actually delivered to the airline. It then flew on the carrier's international routes to the main European cities and regular trips to New York also became the machine's responsibility. In 1973 a second machine was received without any delay, while one of the last commercial 707s to be built was delivered to the airline in 1978.

707-3F9C: 20474 (5N-ABJ), 20669 (5N-ABK), 21428 (5N-ANO)

Nile Safaris Aviation*
Based at Khartoum, the airline uses its 707s for cargo flights between Africa and Europe.

707-330C: 20123 (ST-AKW). **707-338C:** 19622 (ST-ALL)

Northwest Orient
Although Northwest was early customer for the 720, the company waited for the availability of the longer range Series 320B before ordering the 707. Unusually the initial batch of five were fitted with a forward cargo door which gave access to the area

normally occupied by seven rows of seats on the left side. A partition parallel with the aisle separated the passengers from the freight and it was in this configuration that the aircraft entered service on Pacific schedules in July 1963. At the time Northwest activities were concentrated in this area, but in 1969 the 707s began to fly on transatlantic flights to London and Amsterdam. These non-stop, long-haul sectors were taken over by DC-10s and 747s during the 1970s, so by 1979 all 707s had departed.

707-351B: 18584/6 (N351US/3US), 18693 (N35-4US), 18710 (N355US), 19633/6 (N377US/80US), 19872 (N381US). **707-351C:** 18746/8 (N356US/58US), 18888/9 (N359US/60US), 18921/2 (N361US/2US), 18964 (N363US), 19034 (N364US), 19163/4 (N365US/6US), 19168 (N36-7US), 19209/10 (N368US/9US), 19263 (N370US), 19411/2 (N371US/2US), 19434 (N373US), 19443 (N374US), 19631/2 (N375US/6US), 19773/7 (N382US/6US), **720-051B:** 18351/6 (N721US/6US), 18381/2 (N730US/3US), 18420/2 (N727US-/9US), 18687/8 (N734US/5US), 18792/3 (N73-6US/7US)

95

Okada Air*

This Nigerian carrier operates both domestic and international charter flights with both passengers and freight. Although most of its activities are handled by One-Elevens, longer sectors are flown by a 707.

707-355C: 19664 (5N-AOQ). **707-365C:** 19590 (5N-AOO)

Olympic Airways*

By no means one of the first 707 customers, but when Olympic wanted to introduce transatlantic services it turned to Boeing for its equipment. With two aircraft on strength in May 1966, it was possible for the carrier to start its latest venture on 1 June by flying from Athens via Rome and Paris to New York. While its original 707s were brand new, its 720s came from Northwest and were used to replace the older piston-engined types still in service on domestic services. This source also supplied an

Above:
Okada Air took delivery of the ex-ZAS 707-365C SU-DAI in the spring of 1988, whereupon it became 5N-AOO. *AJW*

additional pair of 707s in 1973. Olympic retired its 720s in 1981, but some of the 707s were still operating on scheduled services in the late 1980s although not on the routes they plied originally.

707-351C: 19163/4 (SX-DBP/O). **707-384B:** 20035/6 (SX-DBE/F). **707-384C:** 18948/50 (SX-DBA/C), 19760 (SX-DBD). **720-051B:** 18352/3 (SX-DBG/H), 18355/6 (SX-DBI/K), 18420 (SX-DBL), 18687/8 (SX-DBM/N)

Below:
One of the 707s still serving with Olympic is SX-DBF. *A. S. Wright*

Ontario Worldwide

As the name suggests the airline's two 707s roamed far and wide when operating IT charter flights, the first departure taking place on 1 December 1978. Under two years later operations were ceased due to financial problems resulting in the company's bankruptcy in January 1981.

707-338C: 19623 (C-GRYN). **707-351C:** 18746 (C-GRYO)

Pacific Northern

A long established airline, Pacific Northern operated three 720s on its Seattle to Anchorage route after the first was delivered in 1962. All were transferred to Western Airlines when this carrier absorbed the smaller carrier in 1967.

720-048: 18042 (N7081). **720-062:** 17376/7 (N720V/W)

Pacific Western

Worldwide charters were the main employment for several 707s operated between 1967 and 1979, an activity which ceased with the disposal of the last machine.

707-138B: 17696 (C-FPWV), 17700 (C-FPWW). **707-324C:** 18826 (C-FPWZ). **707-351C:** 18746 (C-FPWJ)

Pakistan International Airlines*

A 707 was used for the Karachi-London route from March 1960 but was joined by the first of the airline's 720Bs in February 1962. The latter type was also employed on the carrier's transatlantic services until the arrival of 707s in 1966. Domestic services with the 720s were interrupted in the mid-1960s due to a war with India, a disagreement which was revived in 1971 eventually to result in the creation of Bangladesh. Services were no longer flown between the two parts of Pakistan so some of the 720s were leased out, but were often re-registered on their return.

707-321: 17601 (N723PA). **707-323C:** 19576 (AP-BBK). **707-340C:** 19284/5 (AP-AUN/O), 19286 (AP-AUP/AXA), 19866 (AP-AVL/AWY), 20275 (AP-AWB/AXZ), 20487 (AP-AVZ), 20488 (AP-AWA/AXG). **707-351B:** 19635 (AP-BAA), 19636 (AP-AZW). **707-373C:** 18991 (AP-AWU), 19441 (AP-AWV), 19715 (AP-AWE), 19716 (AP-AWD). **720-040B:** 18378/80 (AP-AMG/H/J), 18745 (AP-ATQ). **720-047B:** 18062 (AP-AXQ), 18250 (AP-AZP), 18589 (AP-BAF), 18590 (AP-AXK), 18749 (AP-AXM), 18818 (AP-AXL). **720-048:** 18043 (EI-ALC)

Pan American

As the launch customer for the 707, there is no doubt that the airline played a considerable part in the subsequent success of the type. Gradually the company's livery was carried on routes around the world on aircraft in both passenger and cargo configuration. As new models were developed by

Below:
Pacific Western operated the Series 351C C-FPWJ on transatlantic charters. *AJW*

Boeing, so the carrier became the first to place an order. It was therefore not surprising that so many of the world's airlines later flew 707s which had started their careers with Pan American.

707-121: 17586 (N708PA), 17587 (N707PA), 17588/91 (N709PA/12PA). **707-139:** 17903/4 (N778PA/9PA). **707-321:** 17592/605 (N714PA/27PA), 17606/8 (N728PA/30PA), 18083/5 (N757PA/59PA). **707-331:** 17674 (N701PA), 17677 (N702PA), 17680 (N703PA), 17683 (N704PA), 17686 (N705PA), 17689 (N706PA). **707-321B:** 18335/9 (N760PA/64PA), 18832/41 (N401PA/10PA), 18842 (N412PA), 18956/60 (N414PA/18PA), 19264/6 (N419PA/21PA), 19275/8 (N422PA/5PA), 19361/3 (N426PA/8PA), 19364/6 (N433PA/5PA), 19374 (N453PA), 19376 (N454PA), 19378 (N455PA), 19693/9 (N491PA/7PA), 20019/26 (N880PA/7PA), 20027/34 (N890PA/7PA). **707-321C:** 18579/80 (N765PA/6PA), 18591 (N767PA), 18714/8 (N790PA/4PA), 18765/7 (N795PA/7PA), 18790 (N798PA), 18824 (N799PA), 19267/74 (N445PA/52PA), 19367/73 (N457PA/63PA), 19375 (N473PA), 19377 (N474PA), 19379 (N475PA), 20016/8 (N870PA/2PA). **720-023B:** 18033 (N780PA), 18036/7 (N781PA/2PA). **720-030B:** 18057 (N783PA), 18059/60 (N784PA/5PA), 18248 (N786PA), 18250/1 (N787PA/8PA)

Pan Aviation*
This carrier flies regular worldwide services from its Miami base with a particular emphasis on destinations in South and Central America. Aircraft are also operated on behalf of Millon Air, a company undertaking similar work at the Florida airport.

707-321C: 19370 (N720GS), 19373 (N722GS), 19377 (N721GS). **707-337C:** 19212 (N851MA). **707-355C:** 19986 (N723GS). **720-047B:** 18452 (N92GS)

Paninternational
Until December 1969 this German airline was known as Panair and was formed in order to supply the needs of the IT market. To expand this business the company acquired a pair of 707s in November 1970, but their careers were short-lived because the airline went into liquidation at the end of the following year.

707-123B: 17637/8 (D-ALAM/L)

Pelican Air Transport
Operations began in July 1978 when Pelican's 707 flew from the carrier's Manchester base to Zambia. Thereafter the company continued to fly freight charters to Africa, later expanding the coverage to include Hong Kong and India. This came to an end in July 1981 when the airline ceased trading.

707-321C: 19271 (G-BEVN), 19367 (G-BPAT)

Below:
This 707 freighter was given the then out-of-sequence registration G-BPAT when it joined Pelican Air Transport in the late 1970s, which transpired to be a brief career with the short-lived carrier. *Pelican*

Phoenix Airways

Basle became the base of this Swiss company when formed in October 1970 to operate IT charter flights. One 707 was leased from Israeli Aircraft Industries but this was returned at the end of the summer season. A similar machine was then purchased which continued in service until the demise of the company in March 1974.

707-131: 17659 (N732TW), 17671 (HB-IEG)

Pluna (Uruguay)*

Pluna acquired a single 707 in 1981 for use on its international services. Most of these are restricted to South American countries, but the airline also includes Madrid in its network. A second 707 was leased in 1988.

707-321B: 20029 (N729Q). **707-387B:** 19239 (CX-BNU)

Pointair

Non-scheduled passenger services were begun in 1981, operating from Basle to destinations in India, the Far East and North America. In addition to DC-8s, one 707 was used until the company suspended operations in December 1987. The carrier was also associated with the Upper Volta company, Naganagani.

707-321B: 18837 (F-BSGT)

Ports of Call/Skyworld Airlines

Ports of Call was established in 1968 as a travel club to operate group affinity charters plus domestic and international services for its many thousands of members. In September 1986 the carrier was

Above:
One of the Qantas 707-138B fleet, VH-EBL served with the carrier for five years or so before joining Braniff. *Boeing*

renamed Skyworld Airlines although its activities remained unchanged until operations were suspended in July 1989 and the aircraft sold.

707-123B: 17639 (N701PC), 17645 (N702PC), 19335 (N703PC). **707-321B:** 18839 (N454PC). **707-323B:** 20170 (N708PC), 20171 (N910PC), 20172 (N711PC), 20175 (N709PC), 20176 (N712PC), 20177 (N706PC), 20178 (N457PC). **707-323C:** 19587 (N705PC).

Qantas

An early operator of the 707, Qantas introduced its short-bodied Series 138s on to the Sydney-San Francisco route in July 1959. In 1961 the airline followed American's example and progressively returned the machines to Boeing for conversion to -138Bs. This model continued with Qantas until 1968 when the larger -338Cs were delivered. During their career with the carrier, the 707s were responsible for opening up a number of new routes or extending those already flown.

707-138: 17696/702 (VH-EBA/G) – all converted to -138B. **707-138B:** 18067/9 (VH-EBH/J), 18334 (VH-EBK), 18739/40 (VH-EBL/M). **707-338C:** 18808/10 (VH-EBN/P), 18953/5 (VH-EBQ/S), 19293/5 (VH-EBT/V), 19296/7 (VH-EBW/X), 19621/30 (VH-EAA/J). **707-349C:** 19354 (VH-EBZ)

Quebecair

A 707 was ordered for delivery in 1969, but before this stage the aircraft was sold to Wardair. Five years later two secondhand specimens were purchased from American for use on the carrier's IT and charter services to the Caribbean, Hawaii, Europe and North Africa. Both machines left the company in 1979.

707-396C: 20043 (CF-QBG). **707-123B:** 17647 (C-GQBG), 17650 (C-GQBH)

Royal Air Maroc*

With the arrival of the first 707 in 1975 the airline was able to introduce transatlantic services to New York, Montreal and Rio de Janeiro. When the type was eventually replaced on these sectors, the two survivors were then converted into freighters.

707-328: 17619 (CN-RMD), 18375 (CN-RMA). **707-351C:** 19773/4 (CN-RMB/C)

Sabena

Early in 1960 Sabena introduced its new 707s on to several routes to North America and South Africa. Later in the year the airline was involved in the evacuation of civilians from the Congo and it was during these operations that one 707 managed to lift 293 passengers plus 10 crew. Interestingly it was configured with 188 seats. By 1982 the surviving 707s were either operated on IT and charter flights or had been converted as freighters.

707-329: 17623/27 (OO-SJA/E), 18374 (OO-SJF), 18460 (OO-SJG), **707-329C:** 18890 (OO-SJH), 19162 (OO-SJJ), 19211 (OO-SJK), 19996 (OO-SJL), 20198/200 (OO-SJM/O)

Safair*

Both passenger and freight charter flights have been operated by the company since it was formed in 1969. In November 1989 it supplied a 707 on lease to the new South African Airways subsidiary, Skybird, which is operating passenger services in South Africa.

707-323C: 19577 (ZS-LSH). **707-328C:** 19723 (ZS-LSJ), 19917 (ZS-LSK). **707-344C:** 19706 (ZS-LSL), 20283 (ZS-LSF)

Saudia

For some years after 1961 Saudia operated two 720Bs on its services to a number of points in the Middle East, India and North Africa. The type added London to its busy schedule in May 1967, but in 1968 the pair were joined by the first 707. More arrived at intervals until Saudia took delivery of two late production machines in 1977. It was another 10 years before the type was finally withdrawn and made available for sale.

Below:
Although it retained its Sabena ownership, OO-SJF spent some of its time on lease to other carriers until it joined the Israeli Air Force in 1977. *Sabena*

707-368C: 19809/10 (HZ-ACC/D), 21103/4 (HZ-ACG/H), 21261 (HZ-ACI), 21367/8 (HZ-ACJ/K). **707-373:** 18582/3 (HZ-ACE/F). **720-068B:** 18165/6 (HZ-ACA/B)

Scibe-Airlift*
Formed in 1979, Scibe is the largest carrier in Zaire and now provides extensive domestic scheduled and charter services. Worldwide cargo flights are operated with its 707s.

707-321B: 19266 (9Q-CBL). **707-329C:** 20200 (9Q-CBS/9Q-CBW)

Scimitar Airlines
Cargo operations with two 707s began in July 1978 from Gatwick, but were terminated in 1980 following financial difficulties.

707-321C: 18717 (G-BGIS), 18718 (G-BFZF)

Top:
After 18 years of service, Saudia retired HZ-ACD in March 1986.

Above:
This somewhat anonymous 707 is actually operated by the Zaire company Scibe-Airlift as 9Q-CBL.
G. W. Pennick

Seaboard World
Although already essentially a DC-8 operator, Seaboard decided to replace its CL-44s with 707s. The first was delivered in February 1968 followed by a second two weeks or so later. In August both these and the last of the three-strong order were sold to Varig, although Seaboard arranged to lease two back until February/March 1969 whereupon DC-8s resumed their role as mainstay.

707-345C: 19840/2 (N7321S/3S)

Above:
Towards the end of the 1970s Scimitar began cargo operations with a pair of 707s, one of which was -321C G-BFZF. Later this aircraft became G-BNGH with Tradewinds. *AJW*

Shanghai Airlines*
This Chinese independent airline was formed in 1985 to undertake passenger charter work.

707-324C: 19352/3 (B-2423/2). **707-327C:** 19530 (B-2424). **707-338C:** 19294 (B-2426). **707-347C:** 19964 (B-2425)

Sierra Leone Airlines
The present company began international sched-ules to London and Paris in 1982, later expanding to take in the Canaries and points in West Africa. Royal Jordanian supplied the support and the single 707, an arrangement which was ended in 1987 with the suspension of services.

707-384C: 18948 (JY-AEB). **720-030B:** 18251 (9L-LAZ)

Singapore International Airways (SIA)
See Malaysian-Singapore Airlines

Skystar International
From 1982, until it suspended its activities in February 1987, the carrier operated group affinity charters with 707s to link a number of US cities with European centres.

707-321B: 20025 (N728Q), 20029 (N729Q), 20031 (N731Q), 20032 (N895SY), 20034 (N732Q). **707-351C:** 19631 (N 2215Y)

Skyworld Airlines
See Ports of Call

Sobelair
Formed in 1946 as a charter airline, Sobelair used a number of 707s leased from its parent company Sabena. In addition several others were operated independently by Sobelair during the course of its extensive IT activities.

707-328: 17921 (OO-SBR). **707-344:** 17930 (OO-SBW). **707-373C:** 19442 (OO-SBU)

Somali Airlines*
It was 1980 before the airline progressed to the 707 having previously used 720s on its main routes. These are mainly within Africa although services to both Rome and Frankfurt are also flown. Most of the 707's duties have now been taken over by an A310.

707-330B: 19315/6 (60-SBS/T). **707-338C:** 18953/4 (60-SBM/N). **720-023B:** 18013 (60-SAU), 18015 (60-SAW), 18031 (60-SAX)

South African Airways (SAA)
It was mid-1960 when SAA took delivery of the first of three 707s which enabled the airline to introduce the type on the London schedule in October. Political pressures forced the company to reroute its European services via the Canaries and Lisbon, but although frequencies suffered to some extent, the operation continued uninterrupted. A Johannesburg-Perth, Australia, route was also launched using Mauritius and Cocos Islands for transit stops. Many of the long-haul sectors were flown by 747s from the early 1970s, but a few 707s remained with the carrier until 1982.

707-344: 17928/30 (ZS-CKC/E later reregistered ZS-SAA/C). **707-344B:** 18891 (ZS-DYL/ZS-SAD), 19133 (ZS-EKV/ZS-SAE). **707-344C:** 19705 (ZS-EUW), 19706 (ZS-EUX/ZS-SAF), 20110 (ZS-SAG), 20230 (ZS-SAH), 20283 (ZS-SAI)

Southern Air Transport*

Since the airline started operations in 1947, it has specialised in freight work. It was not until the mid-1980s that the company expanded its Hercules fleet to include hush-kitted 707s for its scheduled and charter services.

707-311C: 19789 (N524SJ). **707-321C:** 20016 (N527SJ). **707-338C:** 19621 (N526SJ). **707-369C:** 20084 (N525SJ), 20085 (N528SJ), 20546 (N523SJ)

Southern Cross

Based at Kuala Lumpur, the airline was formed in 1971 to operate worldwide IT and charter flights. Pan American was one of the major shareholders in the company and it was from this source that Southern Cross purchased its first 707. In fact it was destined to be its only aircraft because before a second could be delivered all operations ceased in April 1972.

707-321: 17592 (9M-AQD)

Standard Airways

This American supplemental carrier ceased its operations in February 1964 but was able to resume in 1966 after a general reorganisation. This time more ambitious plans called for four 707s to fly the company's various charter flights. For much of the time several of the aircrafts' careers were punctuated by sub-leases, but this all came to an abrupt halt in August 1969 when Standard once again ceased trading, a situation from which there was no recovery.

707-138B: 17697/8 (N790SA/1SA), 17701 (N792SA), 17700 (N793SA)

Sud Flug

Stuttgart-based Sud Flug International was formed in order to provide transatlantic charter flights. Two ex-Swissair DC-8s were due for delivery at the end of 1967, but in the meantime one 707 was leased from Standard Airways.

707-138B: 17698 (N791SA)

Sudan Airways*

When the carrier's Comets were in need of replacement in the early 1970s, the airline ordered two 707s from Boeing. As an interim measure a similar number were leased from British Midland to maintain the schedules to such European centres as London and Frankfurt. The type has continued this duty although subsequently the fleet grew to five examples.

707-321: 17597 (G-AYBJ), 18083 (G-AYVE). **707-330B:** 18931 (ST-NSR). **707-330C:** 20123 (ST-AKW). **707-368C:** 21104 (ST-DRS). **707-369C:** 20086 (ST-AIX). **707-3J8C:** 21169/70 (ST-AFA/B)

Below:

When Kuwait Airways was disposing of its 707s in the mid-1980s Sudan Airways purchased 9K-ACL, whereupon it became ST-AIX with its new owner. *AJW*

Above:
After using several British Midland 707s for a time, Sudan Airways acquired its own aircraft, ST-AFA being delivered in 1974.

Sun D'Or International Airlines

El Al renamed its charter carrier in September 1981. Non-scheduled passenger flights are operated to Europe and the US with 707s transferred from the parent as required although at one time several carried the airline's title.

707-358C: 19004 (4X-ATR), 20301 (4X-ATY)

Sunrise Airlines/InterAm

This was the trading name for a number of companies involved in providing passenger charter flights between the UK and US. Its own aircraft was not ready for the inaugural trip on 29 July 1982, so Sabena was contracted to supply a 707. This duly carried a load of travellers to Florida, but before they returned home the sun had already set on the airline. InterAm also used the Sunrise 707 and in fact doubled the number of flights completed before also disappearing from the scene.

707-351C: 19209 (N29796)

Syrian Arab Airlines

In the 1970s Syrian Arab leased 707s from British Midland and British Airtours on a number of occasions but never possessed any of its own.

707-321: 17597 (G-AYBJ), 19598 (G-AYVG), 17602 (G-BAEL), 17608 (G-AYXR), 18083 (G-AYVE). **707-436:** 17703 (G-APFB), 17713 (G-APFL)

TAAG Angola*

After the country gained its independence in 1975 the carrier expanded its international schedules and now flies to Cuba, Paris, Rome, East Berlin, Lisbon and Moscow in addition to African cities. A number of 707s are employed for the longer routes while two (D2-TOG and D2-TOU) are operated as freighters by the subsidiary company, Angola Air Charter.

Below:
Israeli charter company Sun D'Or International applied its titles to 707-358C 4X-ATY on lease from El Al in 1982. *AJW*

707-321C: 18881 (D2-TOV). **707-347C:** 19963 (D2-TAM/D2-TOL), 19965 (D2-TAL/D2-TOM). **707-349C:** 18975 (D2-TAC/D2-TOI), 19355 (D2-TAD/D2-TOJ). **707-351C:** 18964 (D2-TOU). **707-373C:** 18583 (D2-TAG/D2-TOG). **707-382B:** 20136 (D2-TOP)

Tampa Airlines Colombia*

Formed in 1974, the company began operations using DC-6s for its freight services. By 1981 Tampa had progressed to 707s and this type has subsequently been used for the scheduled cargo trips to Miami from both Bogata and Medellin. Charter work is also undertaken.

707-321: 17602 (HK-2477). **707-321C:** 18714 (HK-3333), 18717 (HK-3232). **707-324C:** 18886 (HK-2600/HK-3355X). **707-338C:** 18808 (HK-3030). **707-373C:** 18707 (HK-2401)

Top:
After 10 years or so with the Portuguese company TAP, one-time Caledonian Series 399C CS-TBH was sold in America in 1983. *AJW*

Above:
Used for many years by the Portuguese carrier TAP for its international routes, towards the end of their service some of the airline's 707s were used for IT work, as in the case of -382B CS-TBC.
G. W. Pennick

TAP-Transportes Aereos Portugueses (Air Portugal/Air Atlantis)

TAP's South American route was the first to benefit from the delivery of a 707 in 1966, but before long the airline was using the type on the New York and South African sectors. Although later and larger types subsequently joined the airline, a number of 707s continued in service until 1988 by flying on

some of the European schedules or operating IT charters for the associate company, Air Atlantis.

707-382B: 18961/2 (CS-TBA/B), 19740 (CS-TBC), 19969 (CS-TBD), 20136 (CS-TBE), 20297/8 (CS-TBF/G). **707-399C:** 19415 (CS-TBH), 19767 (CS-TBI). **707-373C:** 19179 (CS-TBJ). **707-3F5C:** 20514/5 (CS-TBT/U)

Tarom*

The Romanian carrier was able to expand its international service in 1975 when its new 707s arrived. Two specimens are still in use for passenger services with another pair configured as freighters.

707-321C: 19272 (YR-ABM), 19379 (YR-ABN). **707-3K1C:** 20803/5 (YR-ABA/C)

Tradewinds*

After its first commercial flight in April 1969, Gatwick-based Tradewinds developed its cargo services to serve various points in Africa plus a weekly sortie to Chicago. The first of four 707s

Above:
This ex-Pan American -321C has been with the Romanian airline Tarom since 1976, for much of the time as a freighter registered YR-ABN. *AJW*

arrived in 1977 which then continued in service until the carrier was forced to suspend operations in January 1986. A new start was made in May under new ownership, this time using one hush-kitted 707 (G-BNGH) for the same type of work but with its UK base moved to Stansted. A second machine (G-AWHU) was acquired in 1989.

707-321C: 18717 (G-TRAD), 18718 (G-BNGH). **707-323C:** 18689 (G-WIND), 18690 (G-SAIL), 18691 (G-BFEO). **707-379C:** 19821 (G-AWHU)

Below:
Trans Mediterranean Airways has employed 707s for its worldwide freight work for many years. The windowless OD-AGD is seen awaiting its next consignment at Ostend. *AJW*

Trans Arabian Air Transport*

Founded in 1983, the airline undertakes regular cargo flights within Africa plus general charters to Europe.

707-321C: 19367 (ST-ALM). **707-338C:** 19295 (ST-ALP). **707-349C:** 18976 (ST-ALK)

Trans Asian

See Air Transcontinental.

Transavia Holland

Charter and IT flights were begun in 1966 from Maastricht but Schiphol became the airline's base in 1968. During the peak periods of 1968 and 1970 it was necessary to lease 707s to meet the demands of the Dutch travellers. This led to Transavia purchasing its own machine from American Airlines in 1972 which was then used on the longer haul or high density ITs until withdrawn in 1981.

707-123B: 17646 (PH-TVA). **707-327C:** 19107 (PH-TRV). **707-329C:** 20198 (PH-TVK). **707-355C:** 19664 (PH-TRF). **707-365C:** 19416 (PH-TRW)

Transbrazil*

In 1985 the Brazilian carrier began to assemble a large fleet of 707s for use on its extensive cargo network throughout South America plus the busy link with Miami which was first flown in 1978. For most the stay was short, being replaced by 767s.

707-321C: 20018 (PT-TCR). **707-323C:** 19517 (PT-TCL), 19519 (PT-TCK), 20088 (PT-TCN). **707-327C:** 19529 (PT-TCJ). **707-330C:** 18932 (PT-TCO), 19317 (PT-TCM). **707-336B:** 20456 (PT-TCQ). **707-349C:** 19354 (PT-TCS). **707-365C:** 19416 (PT-TCP)

Above:
Although repainted in Transavia's full livery, 707-327C PH-TRV was on lease from Braniff in the early 1970s. *AJW*

Trans Caribbean

While providing both scheduled and charter services with a fleet of DC-8s, during the winter of 1967 the airline found it necessary to increase its capacity on the busy New York-Caribbean flights by leasing a 707 and 720 from Aer Lingus. There were no further instances before the carrier was taken over by American Airlines in 1970.

707-348C: 19410 (N8789R). **720-048:** 18043 (N7890R)

Trans European Airways

In response to a growing holiday market, Trans European was formed at Brussels in October 1970. Operations began with one 720 in 1971, increasing to two during the next year. These in turn were joined by no fewer than three 707s for the 1974 season, all being employed on IT work. Gradually as new equipment was received the machines were retired, although in 1984 a series 328C was acquired which then served until sold at the end of 1988.

707-131: 17659 (OO-TEC), 17665/6 (OO-TED/E). **707-328C:** 19291 (OO-TYC). **720-025:** 18155 (OO-TEA). **720-048:** 18043 (OO-TEB)

Trans Mediterranean Airways (TMA)*

Along with MEA, TMA endures the constant problems associated with Beirut. Regular 707 freight services were begun in 1970 and in the following year the carrier inaugurated the first round-the-world cargo route from its home base. From Beirut the flight served South East Asia before

reaching Tokyo and the onward trip across the Pacific to New York via Anchorage. After the transatlantic crossing European centres were visited prior to the completion of the trip back in the Lebanon. TMA's fleet still consists entirely of 707s and seems unlikely to change until the risks of damage or destruction at Beirut have receded.

707-321C: 19269 (OD-AGO), 19274 (OD-AGP).
707-323C: 18938 (OD-AGN), 18939 (OD-AGD).
707-327C: 19104 (N7095/OD-AGX), 19105 (N7096/OD-AGY), 19107/8 (OD-AFX/Y), 19440 (N7100/OD-AGW), 19531 (N7104/OD-AGZ).
707-331C: 19213 (OD-AGT), 19214 (OD-AGS).
707-348C: 18737 (EI-AMW)

Trans Polar Airlines
A trio of 720s were acquired by this Norwegian airline in 1970 in order to win a share of the growing tourist industry. Sadly the latter had to manage without the assistance of Trans Polar because in May 1971 the company became bankrupt.

720-025: 18158 (LN-TUW). **720-048:** 18041 (LN-TUV), 18043 (LN-TUU)

Trans World Airlines (TWA)
Although several months behind both Pan American and American Airlines, in 1959 TWA was able to introduce non-stop services between New York and California plus intercontinental schedules to Europe. An expanding network took the carrier's 707s to all parts of the world and included some notable long-distance routes. With the award of a transpacific licence the airline was able to offer a daily round-the-world flight in each direction from August 1969. As in the case of the Pan American fleet, when the 707s were withdrawn they found plenty of eager customers in numerous countries.

707-124: 17610 (N70774), 17612 (N70785), 18012 (N74612). **707-131:** 17658/72 (N731TW/45TW). **707-131B:** 18385/91 (N746TW/52TW), 18392/7 (N754TW/9TW), 18400/4 (N781TW/5TW), 18758/62 (N795TW/9TW), 18986/9 (N6720/3), 19215 (N6724), 19216/9 (N6726/9), 19220/1 (N6763T/4T), 19222 (N6771T), 19223 (N6789T), 19436 (N6790T), 19568/9 (N16738/9), 20056/7 (N86740/1). **707-331:** 17673 (N761TW), 17675/6 (N762TW/3TW), 17678/9 (N764TW/5TW), 17681/2 (N766TW/7TW), 17684/5 (N768TW/9TW), 17687/8 (N770TW/1TW), 17690 (N772TW). **707-331B:** 18405/8 (N773TW/6TW), 18409 (N778TW), 18764 (N779TW), 18913 (N760TW), 18914 (N780TW), 18915 (N793TW), 18916 (N8705T), 18917 (N8715T), 18918 (N8725T), 18978/81 (N18701/4), 18982/5 (N18706/9), 19224/7 (N18710/3), 19570 (N28724), 19571/3 (N28726/8), 20058/67 (N8729/38). **707-331C:** 18711/3 (N786TW/8TW), 18756/7 (N791TW/2TW), 19212/4 (N5771T/3T), 19435 (N5774T), 19566/7 (N15710/1), 20068/9 (N15712/2), 20428/9 (N1793T/4T). **707-373C:** 18709 (N789TW), 18738 (N790TW). **720-051B:** 18381/3 (N791TW/3TW), 18384 (N795TW)

Trek Airways
See Luxair.

Tunis Air
While awaiting the delivery of its new 727s, Tunis Air leased a 707 from Air France in 1970/71 to operate on its longer and higher density routes.

707-328: 17923 (F-BHSP).

Turk Hava Yollari (THY)*
Four 707s were leased by THY in 1971 for use on its busier European routes. This first batch were all Series 321s but in 1974 all were returned to the lessor. From this point the airline's 707 fleet was restocked with some of the earliest airframes which had been modified during their lifetime to -120B standard. These were also employed on the main international sectors until in 1978 the carrier bought three later specimens to replace all others remaining on lease. The trio continued in service until sold in 1985 as a source of spares for USAF KC-135s, while a pair of -321Cs subsequently obtained served as freighters.

707-121B; 17587 (TC-JBA), 17589/91 (TC-JBB/D). **707-138B:** 17697 (TC-JBN), 17701 (TC-JBP). **707-139B:** 17903 (TC-JBE). **707-321:** 17593 (TC-JAH), 17594 (TC-JAN), 17603 (TC-JAJ), 17607 (TC-JAM). **707-321B:** 18834 (TC-JBS), 18835 (TC-JBT), 18842 (TC-JBU). **707-321C:** 18715 (TC-JCC), 19271 (TC-JCF)

Uganda Airlines*
It was in 1977 that Uganda Airlines expanded its activities with the aid of a 707 for cargo charters to Europe. Passenger schedules were developed so that cities in Germany, Italy, Belgium, Egypt and the UK were served, destinations still visited by the airline's remaining 707.

707-321C: 18580 (5X-UAL), 18718 (N795RN), 18765 (SU-BAG). **707-338C:** 19630 (5X-UBC). **707-351C:** 18747 (5X-UAC)

Below:
This 707-351C joined Uganda Airlines as 5X-UAC in May 1980. *AJW*

United Air Lines
Although the airline did not order any 707s, it was the first customer to put the 720 into service in 1960. The type was used extensively on the US domestic routes until the early 1970s when 727/737s took over the duties.

720-022: 17907/17 (N7201U/11U), 18044/50 (N7212U/8U), 18072/82 (N7219U/29U)

United African Airlines
See Jamahiriya Air Transport.

United Arab Airlines
See Egyptair.

Varig*
Two 707s were ordered by the airline at an early stage to enable the type to enter service on the New York-Rio de Janeiro route in mid-1960. A transatlantic route was introduced in 1965 which was later expanded in scope by serving more cities at greater frequencies. Eventually Varig assembled a large fleet of 707s, most of which are now operated as freighters.

707-320C: 20008 (PP-VJH). **707-323C:** 18940 (PP-VLP), 19235 (PP-VLU). **707-324C:** 19177 (PP-VLN), 19350 (PP-VLO), 19869 (PP-VLM), 19870/1 (PP-VLK/L). **707-327C:** 19106 (PP-VLJ).

707-341C: 19320/2 (PP-VJR/T). **707-345C:** 19840/1 (PP-VJY/Z), 19842 (PP-VJX). **707-379C:** 19822 (PP-VJK). **707-385C:** 19433 (PP-VLI). **707-441:** 17905/6 (PP-VJA/B), 18694 (PP-VJJ)

Wardair Canada
In 1962 the airline had its licence amended so that it could participate in international charter work. Two 707s were delivered in 1968 and 1969 which paved the way for transatlantic flights and helped establish the excellent reputation enjoyed by the carrier. Both left Wardair's fleet in 1978 since their duties were by now in the hands of wide-bodied types.

707-311C: 19789 (CF-FAN). **707-396C:** 20043 (CF-ZYP)

West Africa Airline
A licence was awarded in 1977 permitting the carrier to engage in worldwide freight charters. Operations with its sole 707 ended in 1985.

707-336C: 19498 (9G-ACX)

Below:
Once a familiar sight as Wardair's CF-FAN, this Series 311C moved to Kuwait Airways as 9K-ACX in October 1978. Retirement in 1985 took it to the US where it was allocated N524SJ with Southern Air Transport. *Boeing*

Above:
Although painted in World Airlines' livery, the Series 331 N704PA was only leased from Pan American for a short time in 1972. *AJW*

West Coast Airlines
Cargo charter services were begun in July 1982 between Ghana and Europe where Rotterdam was the favourite destination for its pair of 707s. In 1985 the airline disposed of its possessions and now leases freighters as required.

707-331C: 19212 (9G-ACY)

Western Airlines
It was the 720 which was to be the mainstay of Western's early jet fleet although the 707 was not completely absent. The latter type was used to start off the new era services by flying on the Los Angeles-Seattle schedules from June 1960. Nearly 20 years later this route also became the last to be regularly flown by Western's 720s when N3162 completed the journey on 6 January 1980. In the same year all three survivors of the one-time large fleet were withdrawn, a fate also shared by the five 707s.

707-139: 17903/4 (N74613/4). **707-347C:** 19963/7 (N1501W/5W). **720-047B:** 18061/3 (N93141/3), 18167 (N93144), 18451/3 (N93145/7), 18588/90 (N93148/50), 18749 (N93151), 18818 (N93152), 18820 (N93153), 18827/30 (N3154/7), 18963 (N3158), 19160/1 (N3159/60), 19207/8 (N3161/2), 19413/4 (N3163/4), 19438/9 (N3165/6), 19523 (N3167). **720-048:** 18042 (N7081). **720-062:** 18376/7 (N720V/20W)

World Airways
International and domestic charters kept the growing World 707 fleet busy during the mid-1960s, but as the group charter business began to decline so the airline found work for its aircraft by leasing them to other carriers such as Pakistan International and Korean. All 707s had left the airline by the end of the 1970s.

707-331: 17683 (N704PA), 17686 (N705PA). **707-373C:** 18582/3 (N373WA/4WA), 18707 (N375WA), 18991 (N376WA), 19179 (N372WA), 19441/2 (N371WA/70WA), 19715/6 (N369WA/8WA)

Worldways
This Canadian carrier began its long-haul charter work in 1981 when its 707 flew from Toronto to the Azores. A fleet of three was operated for a relatively short time before two left for military service with the Royal Australian Air Force. One remained until 1986 but by then the company was a DC-8 operator.

707-338C: 19623 (C-GRYN), 19629 (C-GGAB). **707-365C:** 19416 (C-GFLG)

Young Cargo
In 1977 the Belgian carrier took delivery of a pair of 707s to take over from its fleet of Britannias. Worldwide cargo charter operations were continued and contract work was undertaken for other airlines, but in July 1979 the company was declared bankrupt and Young Cargo slipped into history.

707-338C: 19621/1 (OO-YCK/L)

Above:
**In the early 1980s Zaire Aero Service operated
707-458 9Q-CPM.** *AJW*

Zaire Aero Services

Formed in 1976 to operate cargo and passenger charters, the airline acquired a 707 in 1980. Its stay was fairly brief since with the takeover of its operator by Katale Aero Transport, the aircraft's services were no longer required.

707-458: 18357 (9Q-CPM)

Zambia Airways*

A DC-8 was used when Zambia Airways started its international routes, but in 1975 the first 707 arrived to take over the duties. Several European cities

Below:
**This ex-Qantas 707-338C has been operated by
Zambia Airways since 1977 as 9J-AEL.**
G. W. Pennick

were served at this time and the network was steadily expanded as more aircraft joined the fleet. Although the trunk routes are now flown by a DC-10, one 707 remains in use on other sectors.

707-321C: 19367 (9J-AEQ). **707-338C:** 19295 (9J-AEL). **707-349C:** 18976 (9J-ADY), 19354 (9J-AEC). **707-351C:** 19263 (9J-AEB)

ZAS Airline of Egypt*

Zarkani Aviation Services launched this carrier in July 1982 in order to provide scheduled and charter cargo flights to Europe from its Cairo base. A fleet of 707s was built up until in 1986 there were six on strength at one time. During 1987 the company was granted a licence to carry passengers with the result that one of the 707s was configured for IT work. This role ended with the delivery of an MD-83 and a pair of leased DC-9s to leave only two 707 freighters on strength in 1989.

707-328C: 19521 (SU-DAB), 19916 (SU-DAA). **707-336C:** 19843 (SU-DAC), 20517 (SU-DAD). **707-338C:** 19590 (SU-DAI), 19621/2 (SU-DAF/E)